To Lis[...]

Thanks for Always
Being there 2
help —

Cheers

HUNTING ACROSS THE DANUBE

Advance Praise

"Peter's words ring true to the spirit of Romania and Hungary. Having spent almost thirty years living each hunting season from the Puszta to the Carpathians is quite evident in this authoritative work."

—Cavaliere Ugo Gussalli Beretta, president of Beretta

"Of all the great game lands across the planet from Alaska to Africa, none offer the pageantry and history of that found in Hungary. And no one knows more about this country's unforgettable stalking and shooting than Peter Horn. For him, hunting is an immersion into culture that binds sportsmen around the world even if they do not share a language. He is, quite simply, the American hunting ambassador to one of Europe's most spectacular sporting destinations."

—Chris Dorsey, president of Orion Entertainment

"Peter Horn has the soul of a hunter and the heart of a lion. On my over twenty safaris to Africa, I always preferred to go one-on-one, unless I was hunting with Peter. He is one of the most traveled and knowledgeable big–game hunters extant."

—Alex Brant, founding president of the tristate chapter of Safari Club International, author of *The Complete Guide to Wing Shooting*

"There is not a better outdoor experience than with the hunt master himself. His incredible eastern European adventures offer the finest in nature, wildlife, accommodations, cuisine, and camaraderie. Turn back the clock and experience grand hunts of the past in this unspoiled part of the world."

—Joseph P. Clayton, president and CEO of DISH Network

"One of the pioneers of the post-Ceaușescu hunting era."

—Petre Gărgărea, head of the Romanian hunting department

"Peter's knowledge of European hunting traditions and his love of the hunt make a trip magical, which is evident in this book."

—Brenda Potterfield, co-owner of MidwayUSA

"There is no one who knows so well the Hungarian hunting regions and games as Peter Horn. It was no accident that he has received the Hubertus Cross and the Pro-Turismo Awards. Peter's book provides a great experience for all of us. He takes us on a journey around the Carpathian Basin's enchanting landscapes and wonderful hunting challenges. I am convinced that his readers are not only going to have a lot of fun but sooner or later will visit Hungary as well."

—Dr. Zoltán Budai, director of the Hungarian National Tourist Office in New York

"Some people are excellent hunters. Some writers can capture the passion of the hunt. Rare is the person who can do both. Peter Horn is one of those rare people. The hunter that finds joy in the literature of the hunt will be richly rewarded by savoring the pages of Mr. Horn's latest contribution to this inspiring genre."

—Michael G. Sabbeth, ethics lawyer and author of *The Good, The Bad & The Difference*

HUNTING ACROSS THE DANUBE

Through Fields, Forests, and Mountains of Hungary and Romania

BY

Peter Lewis Horn II

Skyhorse Publishing

Skyhorse Publishing books may be purchased in bulk at special discounts for sales promotion, corporate gifts, fund-raising, or educational purposes. Special editions can also be created to specifications. For details, contact the Special Sales Department, Skyhorse Publishing, 307 West 36th Street, 11th Floor, New York, NY 10018 or info@skyhorsepublishing.com.

Skyhorse® and Skyhorse Publishing® are registered trademarks of Skyhorse Publishing, Inc.®, a Delaware corporation.

Visit our website at www.skyhorsepublishing.com.

10 9 8 7 6 5 4 3 2 1

Library of Congress Cataloging-in-Publication Data is available on file.

Cover design by Jane Sheppard
Cover photo credit Toni Török

Print ISBN: 978-1-62914-187-9
Ebook ISBN: 978-1-62914-321-7

Printed in China

THE PHILOSOPHY OF
HUNTING ACROSS THE DANUBE

This is the first book written in English about two of Eastern Europe's premier hunting destinations. The book is animated by my desire to share this little-known sporting paradise with educated hunters. The chapters detail game I have hunted over the past three decades, including stag, boar, roebuck, bear, wolf, chamois, capercaillie, pheasant, mouflon, and duck, in areas that regularly produce world-class trophies yet remain unknown amongst the most experienced hunters. The hunting culture and traditions of Romania and Hungary, which figured so prominently in the Austro-Hungarian Empire, profoundly influenced the development of European and international hunting. By sharing the latest facts about the finest hunting areas, seasons, firearms, and equipment, I hope to awaken an appreciation for all the best that Hungary and Romania offer sportsmen.

The water is not only for sheep.

ABOUT THE AUTHOR

Peter Lewis Horn II is an international hunter, outdoorsman, and conservationist. Since 1991, he has been the senior partner in Pannonvad, a Budapest company that organizes and leads hunting trips across Hungary and Romania. Mr. Horn has hunted extensively in Hungary since 1985 and in Romania from the moment the country was reopened to sportsmen in 1990. In the same year, Mr. Horn was the first American sportsman invited by the national government to hunt Romania's famed Timisoara region after Nicolae Ceauşescu's reign of terror ended. Mr. Horn formerly worked as professional hunter in Africa and served as the President of Safari Club International Conservation Fund (SCICF). He is the Vice President of Beretta USA's Retail Division, General Manager of Beretta Gallery Expeditions, and the author of many articles and book chapters on hunting throughout the world. Mr. Horn is a member of the International Order of St. Hubertus, the Order of St. Hubertus of Hungary, a Fellow of the Explorers Club, and in November of 2013 received the Pro Turismo Award from the Minister of Economic Affairs in the Hungarian Parliament for his twenty-five years of bringing hunters to Hungary and promoting its tourism.

Waiting for our last pheasant.

Table of Contents

Acknowledgments

Hunting is often a solitary profession. There are lodges, the fellowship of the hunt, and the camaraderie of time well spent in the field, but hunting is ultimately about an individual, nature, and that moment of truth when the trigger breaks the silence. We hunters love to be amongst the wild things, but we live with people who know that hunting season often means long absences unless one is as fortunate as I am to be married to someone who shares the passion. My wife, Debbie, has supported my obsession for hunting and been my partner on adventures from the far corners of the Sudan to the cozy fields of Hungary. She is an integral part of the foundation of this book. She edited each and every page, and this work is as much hers as mine.

My mom, Mickey, always understood my need to wander among wild things. I am most thankful for that.

Toni Török, my partner in Pannonvad, helped ignite my love affair with Eastern Europe that is now in its third decade. Without Toni's expertise, this book and so much else would never have been possible.

Cavaliere Ugo Gussalli Beretta gave me the tools to develop American hunting in Hungary and Romania. Thank you, my boss and my friend, from the bottom of my heart.

A special acknowledgment has to go to my assistant, Elizaveta Lim, who worked closely with me to make sure this book would be an authoritative guide, and to my new shooting buddy Steven M. Sears, who helped refine this work into easy reading.

My son, Lee Phips Horn, has accompanied me on many of my most rewarding hunts. Helping him develop into a fine shot and a sporting gentleman is my greatest accomplishment. With tradition as a driving force, Lee gave me a continued reason to finish this book. I will never forget him saying over and over, "Dad, you should really write a book!"

To Jay Cassell, for his continued support at Skyhorse Publishing.

To Baron Carlo Amato, who was the first to kindle my constant quest for wild boar. I thank you.

To Zoltan Boros for the excellent sketches and Dusan Smetana for his fine photos of the driven wild boar hunt.

To my New York staff, including Ed Anderson and Scott Cummings, who helped with the firearm details.

I could not have completed this work without the help of Zoltan Budai of the Hungarian Tourist Board or Dr. Gyula Varga of SEFAG. Also, many, many thanks to H.R.H. Juan Carlos of Spain, Alan Romney, Dr. Marinos Petratos, Steven Weiss, Gentry Beach, Bill Schaefer, Chris Wyatt, Alain Boucheron, Barbara and Alan Sackman, Bob and Sylvia Rafford, Tom Hicks Jr., Lee Kaufman, Steve Barasch, Bob Hoover, Don Trump Jr., Bruno and Charles Bich, Lodovico Antinori, Adam and Tim Fenton, Floyd and Michael Hatch, and "Uncle" Bill Schaefer. To all the friends and hunters who spent time with me on our numerous trips to some of Eastern Europe's most remote areas, for it was through them and with them that I was able to experience, as if for the first time, my love of this hunting experience again and again.

Many of the author's friends in this photo from twenty-five years ago are still hunting with him today.

Introduction

The Danube is Europe's second largest river. It flows from Germany into Austria, and it winds its way into regions of the European continent that are historically associated with the worst of man and not the best of nature. In the unusual way some things of this world come into existence, the dictatorships that oppressed the people of Eastern Europe created conditions that allowed wildlife to flourish. Many of the world's great hunting traditions come from the countryside of Romania and Hungary, the cradle of the Austro-Hungarian Empire. Though the literature of Romania and Hungary is commemorated in the mother tongues of those great nations, little has been written in English of this hunter's paradise. For more than twenty-five years, I have tried enlightening Americans and sportsmen from dozens of other countries to this singular part of the hunting world.

I owe a debt to my old friend and hunting buddy Angiolo Bellini and his wife, Elisabetta. They first introduced Debbie, my wife, and me to stag hunting in the Zemplen Mountains of Northern Hungary. They showed us a world of untouched European charm. From the first day, the guides, hunting lodges, forests of spruce and oak, and game drew me in. Even now, I can close my eyes and journey back there, because the smells and sights are ingrained in my memory. After more than one hundred hunts, I still discover something new each time I am there.

After that first stag hunt, I met Toni Török. It was 1986. I was on my inaugural driven pheasant shoot that I outfitted. Toni, who speaks six languages, was the line's interpreter. After a brief time talking about our favorite subject, hunting, I found out he worked as a manager for a hunting company in Budapest. He had been a chief hunter in Romania for five years and even hunted with the infamous dictator Nicolae Ceauşescu, who was a fanatical sportsman.

Toni knew everything to know about hunting. He held a degree in silviculture (forestry); he spoke the languages of local hunters and the important client tongues. But two things were stopping him from starting his own business—he needed a partner with contacts in the American market and someone who could provide some seed money. We talked for half an hour, and I willingly provided him with the last two pieces of his puzzle. In the eighties, Hungary was still under communist rule and Romania was closed to outside hunters. Since I already had a booking business in full swing, running trips mostly to Africa, Spain, and the British Isles, and had made a number of expeditions— including fifty or so trips to Africa and a couple dozen to England, Scotland, and the Iberian Peninsula—it was perfect timing for me to learn about an area that so little was known about in America. Soon after that first driven shoot, Toni and I formed Pannonvad, which literally means "Hungarian hunting" in the local tongue.

Tony Lombardo shares the luck of his several Beretta Gallery Expedition Hunts.

In 1990, Romania opened her doors to foreign sportsmen after seventeen years under Ceauşescu's dictatorship. The change marked the start of a wonderful ongoing talk between Toni and me about his days as a boy in the Romanian countryside, where he learned to hunt and fish from his dad. I never got tired of listening to the stories of when Toni was a chief hunter. He painted an exciting picture of hunting in Europe as it existed fifty or sixty years ago. Cut off from the outside world, Romania's wild animals were everywhere. The primitive areas stayed untouched by the usual masses of foreign hunters. I thought it was likely that it would always be that way. But in the spring of 1990, while on a roebuck hunt in Hungary, Toni turned to me and said without any great fanfare, "We leave for Romania in two hours. I finally got the papers for you to be the first American allowed to hunt in the Western part of the country in over twenty-four years." What we found was everything and more than Toni had promised and I had imagined from his stories.

On our first trip, I took three gold and one silver-medal wild boar (I had special dispensation to shoot boar at that time of year) and five medal-class International Council for Game and Wildlife Conservation (CIC) roebucks. The second trip produced one of the largest wild stags ever taken, two huge boars with tusks of more than ten inches, and a silver-medal fallow deer. This was a magical time for any hunter. The amount of game was simply overwhelming. Stag and wild boar were in fields in the middle of the day. Fallow deer in some areas were in herds of one hundred or more. Roe deer were spotted everywhere.

That first year in Romania reminded me of the areas I was fortunate enough to open up in the Sudan. Those pristine swamps, hills, and fields were untouched for years. Animals had no fear of their greatest foe. Of course, nothing in this world lasts forever. The word soon spread about this new frontier, which was made possible by the collapse of the Iron Curtain and the end of dictatorships. First the Italians came, then the rest of Europe and with the help of people such as Bob Kern of the Hunting Consortium and me, Americans followed.

One of the real pleasures of hunting, and especially my profession, is the opportunity to make so many friendships, as well as the joy of hosting famous hunters, such as King Juan Carlos of Spain, Don Trump Jr., the Marquee Lodovico Antinori, Bruno and Charles Bich, General Joe Ralson (former head of NATO Air Forces), Italian Designer Stefano Ricci, Jim Clarke (of Netscape fame), and noted outdoor TV Director Chris Dorsey, just to name a few.

Toni and I have made many lasting friendships on our hunts. It is like family—some have hunted with us eight times or more. On a recent driven pheasant shoot we hosted, nine of the guns had hunted with me sixty-one times in Hungary, Romania, Spain, Scotland, Ireland, and the Czech Republic. There is nothing like listening to old friends tells stories of past hunts to the new guns. For Toni and me, hunting is a passion more than a business. Introducing people to the sport you love most and watching their excitement and enthusiasm grow over time is an experience second to none.

Chapter One

Home of the Mountain Stag

The Zemplen Mountains rise in Northeastern Hungary. They are several hours outside Budapest, a city many travelers think of as the Paris of the East. To reach these mountains requires a drive of several hours through quaint towns, which always remind me of the storybooks I read when I was young. I first came here in 1985 to hunt the stag rut with Angiolo Bellini, one of the world's great gentlemen hunters. We had met in 1985 at the Safari Club International Convention. He was the chairman of the first SCI chapter in Italy. I was asked by SCI to look after the delegation. Soon, the talk naturally turned to hunting. Angiolo, like me, had hunted everywhere from South America to Europe to Africa. When we discussed Europe, I mentioned the only stags I had ever taken were in Spain and Scotland, to which Angiolo answered, "Those are not stags but the baby cousins of the giants of Eastern Europe!"

Now, I can tell you that the stags in Spain and Scotland are considered amongst the world's finest specimens of Western red deer, so I was naturally intrigued. I asked Angiolo if he could find someone in Hungary to take us to these big stags. "I will do more than that," he said, "Why don't you and your wife be my guests during the September rut?"

Soon, Debbie and I found ourselves driving through old-fashioned villages. As we drove higher up into the mountains, the pinewoods and fields yielded glimpses of roebuck and stag. As with seeing any animal, this really stirs the hunter's blood. Upon arriving

The author, Debbie Horn, and their guide, Zoltan, with the author's 270 made by Paul Jaeger on a Sako action, of course.

at the hunting lodge, I could feel that we were about to go on a hunt to remember. The lodge had a great main room with stag trophies all over the walls, complemented by roebuck heads, boar rugs, and a few sets of tusks to round out the display. The building was a bit tired by some Western standards, but the wood-burning fireplace and the balcony overlooking the pristine forest were just right for us. I had no idea that I was starting a more than twenty-five-year love affair learning about hunting in Eastern Europe.

The first morning we ventured out at 5 a.m. with guides we had met the night before. My guide, Zoltan, spoke Hungarian and German, but we had a common tongue—that of the hunter. As we walked the dirt roads along the mountainside, we would step a few yards and stop to listen for the roar of lovesick stags. Then, Zoltan would say in German (as I understood most of the hunter's terms in that language) "too young" or "too small," as he responded to the stags using a call fashioned only from his hands. He perfectly mimicked the voices of rutting stags. I began to learn, as I had after so many years in Africa, to always trust your guide. By 9:30 a.m., we saw four stags. Then,

Zoltan heard a deer he wanted to check out. He told me to wait by some trees and be very quiet. I was daydreaming about a stag when I heard something move about two hundred yards to my right. I hoped it wasn't a big red deer, because I really did not know what qualified as a trophy in Hungary. I was to learn, after many years and looking at hundreds of stags, that you watch for the thickness of the antlers coupled with their height and the length of each tine. The power of an old stag is at the top; look for a good crown with many points.

Peter and Debbie with her first mountain stag.

The noise was now one hundred yards away, and suddenly there appeared a huge wild boar strolling down the trail. After years of taking clients hunting everywhere from the Sudan to Spain, I know you do not pull the trigger when you don't know the rule of a country. I let that three-hundred-pound bad boy pass by with most of his nine-inch tusks shining brightly in the morning sun. Everyone gasped as I retold the story that night over a fine dinner of stag steaks and Hungarian goulash. One guide asked, "Why didn't you shoot? You may not see another boar that size ever again!"

"Better safe than sorry," I replied. Also, I had a feeling this was not going to be my last trip to Hungary. After many safaris to Africa, I was ready for a new frontier.

A True Shot

I do not hunt to collect species. I hunt the same areas many times over to learn about the game, people, and country. That is why I took many bongos in the Sudan. I wanted to become a bongo hunter. I wanted to understand the animal on the level of the locals. Zoltan was a great guide for me. Every day he taught me more about the European stag and, coupled with Angiolo's knowledge plus my past experience, I felt ready to stalk this noble animal. After a few days, I learned to differentiate the sounds of the stag's roaring. The older boy's sound that came from within was much deeper than the young pup's meager attempts. Each day we were able to call these magnificent creatures to within fifty yards. On the second day, Debbie connected with a beautiful stag at one hundred and thirty yards, with a well-placed shot from her Sako .270 Winchester. Elisabetta had her stag on the third day, and Angiolo had his on the fifth. Now, it was up to me to bring in the last trophy. We were having such a great time among ourselves that whether I got a stag almost became secondary.

On the sixth day, Zoltan and I climbed higher up the mountains than we had been before to an area on the Czechoslovakian border. A monster stag called out in the distance just before daybreak. As we made our way through the brush in the dark, I could just make out the silhouette of the red deer. I was raising my rifle when Zoltan signaled, "No!" I asked why, and he pointed in the same direction whispering, "Czechoslovakia." If we shot the animal, we wouldn't be allowed to cross the border to collect him.

"Just my luck," I thought as I put my gun down. We quickly left the old bull and soon heard another one answer him. We stopped and listened every few steps. Zoltan suddenly turned and cupped his hands to his mouth to call the stag. He called back. I raised my rifle just as the sun came through the trees. The light illuminated his magnificent rack as I waited for the signal to shoot.

First, Zoltan mumbled, "Yo," (Hungarian for "good") and then, "Nem" ("no"). It seemed because the deer was in a thicket and we could only see the top of his back, he thought there was no shot. I had a dead rest at eighty yards on an animal whose anatomy I had studied many times. The .270 Winchester I was using had seen hundreds of shots hit practice targets in the kill zone. Before he could protest again, I calmed myself for a shot I knew I could make. The bull fell like a sack of potatoes. Zoltan never saw the hit or the animal go down, for that matter.

After stalking through the thick bush toward where the stag was last seen, we could find nothing—no blood, no hair, and no stag. We traced our steps back to the side of the hill where we felt the deer had last stood. "You missed!" cried Zoltan.

"No way!" I shot back. "I smacked that bull in the spine, and he is stone dead!" Even though the forest on the side of the mountain was thick and steep, I knew I had hit him.

Once again, Zoltan stated, "You missed."

I ran through the events from loading the gun to the actual shot. My answer was still, "No, I hit him. Yo!"

After Zoltan's tenth cigarette of the morning, the wiry old hunter finally made his way down the hill to fetch his tracking dog and a couple of other hunters to search for the stag. I settled up against a tree, took out some water and chocolate, and once again began to think of the shot. I knew it was a true shot. You know when you hit something well—it is different than hoping. Feeling confident, I scrambled to my feet and slowly started down the steep slope into the forest. There, not sixty yards from the lip of the hill, lay the stag with his CIC bronze-medal ten-point rack. What a jubilant moment!

After taking photographs and field dressing the stag, I started back up the hill to a beautiful field of emerald green grass I had spotted by the road when we first trekked in. The sun was glistening through the trees as I leaned against a mighty willow. I could not wait to see the look on Zoltan's face as he discovered the shot placement exactly where I said it would be in German, English, and sign language. Two hours passed before he returned with his dog and two other guides.

As I sat under the beautiful tree looking out over the field into a big valley, I heard another stag roar. Then I heard from the other side of the field an even louder roar answering back. As the roars got closer, I crouched behind my willow. First, a ten-pointer showed himself just at the edge of the field. After looking around ever so cautiously, the bull stepped out onto the grass. From a different area, I could hear an older stag roaring closer. The magnificent sixteen-point red deer barreled out into the field without hesitation, for it was his field. The two stags danced round each other, the younger one never getting too close. Then, the old boy charged the intruder. As they locked antlers, the noise cracked the valley open.

For the next five minutes, I had the rare treat of witnessing a stag fight. It was soon over, as the larger male had the smaller stag down on his front legs. I saw a bit of blood on the young boy's coat as he ran for the hills. The old stag roared again with a different sound. It was a sound of victory. A few minutes later, eleven females strolled into the open, and I knew what the fight was all about.

Angiolo, the author, Debbie, and Elisabetta. Everyone has a stag except for me, with only an apple to display.

By the time Zoltan returned, I was half-asleep beneath my tree. I first saw the dog, then the three hunters hike up the field. I tried explaining the best I could that the stag was already dead, but the dog soon found the old boy and signaled to us in dog language that, indeed, the stag was down. Later that night, Zoltan made a toast to the fact that the first American he had taken on a hunt could actually shoot. I asked Debbie what she remembered best about this adventure, to which she answered, "Everything!" The animals, the breathtaking views, the forests and mountains, the food, the lodges, and the hunting guides all made an indelible impression on her and me. Our first trip to Eastern Europe opened up endless opportunities for new adventures that have lasted into three decades.

Homage to the fallen.

Spanish stag hunting has a beautiful backdrop, with her haciendas, food, and service that rivals the Ritz. In Scotland, you get the beauty of the moors with a country lifestyle that we in the hunting world think of as a perfect setting to hunt the red stag. The Czech Republic has her own flavor that is strongly reminiscent of the German tradition I found in the Eastern part of Deutschland. Slovenia has a unique feeling I found nowhere else. However, the most perfect setting to hunt stag is the mountains of Romania and Hungary. Our first hunt in Hungary, near the Czech border, burned a permanent memory in our minds. I have more than one hundred trips to Eastern Europe under my belt, Debbie has seven, and my son Lee is planning his third trip for next year. My family and friends seem to quickly fall under the spell of Eastern Europe's hunting magic during our adventures. Since then, Pannonvad has organized hundreds of hunts and introduced a countless number of American hunters to "our" special part of this world. We have also run numerous hunts for Hungarian and Romanian hunters, Croatians, French, English, Irish, Lebanese, Germans, Russians, Swiss, Italians, Belgians, Greeks, Spaniards, and hunters from so many other countries who have come to know these forests and mountains.

Chapter Two

The Birthday Boar

In my fiftieth year, I planned to spend as much time hunting as I could before Father Time took over. Dr. Marinos Petratos, my hunting buddy of twenty-odd years, and I decided to hunt wild boar in Hungary's famed Devecser area. We had just finished a successful stag hunt (one gold and one silver, thank you). Toni Török selected the Devecser area of Western Hungary mainly for the large number of huge boar it was known to harbor.

My constant hunting buddy Dr. Marinos Petratos in front of our favorite hunting store (now gone forever) on Castle Hill.

We arrived at our lodge late in the evening, just in time for a delicious supper and some good old stories of the hunt told with great relish by our guides, Jozsef and Miklós. I had my new Beretta 689 double rifle in 9.3x74R shined and ready to go for our first trek at 4:30 in the morning. This is the perfect caliber for big boar. It falls right between the .338 Winchester and the .375 H&H—two of my other favorites. The 9.3x74R is what true European boar aficionados use.

The first morning of our boar hunt began with a stroll through the darkened, dense forest of beautiful pine trees planted neatly in a row. I could not help but think back to my days as master of the hunt at the Shangri-La wild boar preserve in Nova Scotia. The musty smells, deep muddy tracks, and sighting of a big black shadowy hump slowly moving in the dewy gray mist all brought me back to memories of numerous hunts I had taken sportsmen on for this noble animal.

Daylight was just beginning to peek its head through the needled pines when we directed ourselves toward a narrow game trail. A few feet down the path, we saw fresh tracks of a big boar that had crossed the path earlier in the morning. No matter how many times you hunt wild boar, it is the same. The pounding of your heart speeds up, your senses become more acute and alive, and you look for that huge black spot somewhere in the midst of all the green and other shades of the forest. Suddenly, we approached a sounder of three large females, two young males, and a whole bunch of baby boar. After carefully scanning the woods beyond the group, because larger boars tend to hang back by the tree line, we returned to the tracks of the single male. After what seemed like an eternity, but was actually only a couple of hours, Jozsef spotted him. I raised my binoculars to take a better look. My heart sank. The boar was a three-hundred-pound five-year-old with tusks about six inches long. Unfortunately, this small tusker was not what we had come to Eastern Europe to hunt, so after watching him for about fifteen minutes, we quietly moved off and headed back to the lodge for a hearty lunch.

As I recounted my morning hunt, Dr. Marinos asked how I knew the boar had only six-inch tusks. After studying hundreds of male boar, you develop an ability to recognize several telltale signs. Only about one-third of the tusk is outside the jaw. So if you see just more than two inches of ivory, you know they are about six inches overall. Mature males usually have a humped back and his "pencil" is easily spotted without much trouble. The thickness of the tusks also helps make it a first-rate trophy. A big male can weigh anywhere from three to five hundred or more pounds. The biggest one we ever took was six hundred and seventeen pounds with Ken Behring in 2002. What a hog that was! The females can weigh up to four hundred pounds, so you really have to look for the telltale signs of the male closely.

My prodigy Chip Brian with his Beretta 689 and a double taken with his double.

The next three days proved uneventful. We continued dismissing the few big boars that were spotted, as none had tusks that approached eight to ten inches in length. After taking two hundred or so male boar through the years, I did not want just any animal that happened along; I was after a porker to remember! This was my birthday goal.

On the fourth morning, Dr. Marinos made a nice one-hundred-sixty-yard shot on a silver-medal trophy. This was a classic boar hunt. He first spotted a female walking with a few young following and a big boy bringing up the rear. Marinos already had his Sako .30-06 positioned on a tree ready for the shot. The last boar would be his.

It was in the morning of my fifth day searching for my elusive prize that we came upon a family group of boar feeding in a cornfield. We watched silently for twenty minutes or so, but only female and young could be seen. I did not want to continue on, as my hunter's sixth sense was kicking in and forcing me to stay. After another fifteen minutes of hoping for more visitors, we finally saw him. I did not have to ask if I should squeeze the trigger, for he was black, had a massive hump, appeared to be around three hundred and fifty pounds, and had approximately three or four inches of tusk showing. The boar had no idea we were there, so I took my time and found the perfect rest on an old dried-up tree stump about one hundred meters from my target.

My body was calm as my scope's crosshairs found his chest. But just as I squeezed the trigger, he turned away. In my mind he was hit well, although my guide yelled out, "Finish him! Shoot again!" I had seen enough wild boar taken and thought there was no need. He would go down within fifty yards. As we gingerly stalked into the forest, we followed a nice blood trail.

I remember thinking, "It will not be long now." We kept moving ever so slowly, but after a while it became evident that the anchor shot had indeed been needed. We tracked him until the sun faded and the flashlights came out. I thought to myself that a huge wounded boar at night in a thick forest was the perfect scenario for a charge. Having been through more than one mad boar situation in my life, I opted to wait until the next morning. The blood was the right color, and he was already slowing down, so why tempt fate?

After an almost sleepless night of continually filling my head with thoughts and half-guesses of why I did not take the second shot, I wondered why the boar had not gone down right away and if the bullet did not hit a vital area. I could not wait for the morning sun to rise.

At 7 a.m. we were right back on his trail, as we had left behind a white handkerchief for a marker the night before. Now we had a tracking dog and two other guides in our merry little band to aid in our search. The small German Teckel tracked the boar for more than five miles and eventually found the spot where he had laid down for the night. There was so much blood saturating his pine needle bed that I knew he had to be around the corner. The "corner" led us through the woods and another two miles toward the river. I knew the boar could never swim the river and would probably be found just shy of the water. But the persistent little Teckel tracked the boar to the river's edge. This was some birthday present, for I was sure that this mighty lord of the forest had enough strength to just make it into the water and had likely floated miles downstream, lost forever.

A wild boar emerges from the depths of the forest. Illustration by Zoltan Boros

After a moment of feeling sorry for myself, I retraced the hunt over and over again in my mind, all the way from the shot to the dog tracking the boar's scent down to the river. I was certain I hit the boar in the right spot with a big heavy bullet. He had to be finished. I pleaded with Toni, who by now had joined the party, to find us a boat, as this boar must be down on the other side of the river. Finally, after convincing the guides they must take a look, Jozsef admitted that there was a boat owned by some fishermen downstream that we could possibly borrow. Although the suggestion was made that we go back to the lodge and wait, I told everyone I wouldn't budge until they checked out the area on the other side of the river.

Two hours passed before we heard the sound of the boat engine puttering in the distance. Overly anxious, we waited for the guides to disembark and begin their search. To everyone's amazement, they immediately found boar tracks. To the shock of all, not fifty yards into the woods was a gold-medal boar. My boar, taken during my fiftieth year, proved to be one of the largest wild boar taken in Western Hungary in 1986. The tusks measured at more than twenty-five centimeters, or ten inches.

The moral of this story is two-fold. First, ammunition is cheap, so shoot until the animal is down, especially with dangerous game. Second, learn to trust your instincts. I always tell anyone who will listen that if the animal does not go down with the first shot, keep pulling the trigger until it does. I usually listen to my guides without question, but I hesitated because I had become overconfident. However, the doubt and suspense of the hunt gave me an exciting story.

Chapter Three

The Monster of Banloc: Finding One of the Largest Wild Stags Ever Taken

Nicolae Ceauşescu was executed in December of 1989. Romania's long reign of terror was suddenly over, and the people of this ancient nation, once influenced by the Roman and Ottoman empires, quickly established the foundation of a modern country. What was accomplished in such short order is a testament to the vibrancy and passion of a people I have come to know well.

In May of 1990, I was the first American in twenty-four years to hunt in the region outside Timisoara, an elegant city that reminds one of a Bavarian town in Germany. The city is one of the largest in Romania. Although the area is famous for agriculture and the quality of its soil, major companies, including Procter & Gamble, have recently opened offices there. Toni, my partner in Pannonvad, knows the area well. He was a chief hunter in the Timisoara region for ten years. He promised we would be first to hunt this part of the country, as soon as Ceauşescu was gone. He was, and is, a man of his word, and we both discovered opening a region for hunting that was so long closed to outsiders is truly epic.

Up close and personal.

Toni and I were in for the opening week of Hungary's roebuck season in May. It was late—everyone had retired to their rooms for the evening. Suddenly, Toni came into my room. "Pack your bags as fast as you can. We should be at the Romanian border before nightfall." We immediately drove the sixty-five miles to the Romanian border, where the area's hunting mandarins met us. I think that even for them the moment loomed large. Adam Craciunescu, Director of Forestry for Timisoara County, and Dr. Ion Vava, Hunting Inspector of Timisoara County, issued me a gun permit. It was handwritten on a plain piece of paper. No one had brought a hunting rifle through this custom post in many years. No fewer than a dozen officials came to admire my hand-me-down custom pre-'64 Winchester .308, as it was the first many of them had ever seen. I, after decades of hunting all over the world, was about to encounter hunting grounds the likes of which I had never before seen.

We hunted areas so full of game I thought we had somehow stumbled into the mythical fields of and forests of St. Hubertus, the patron saint of hunters. I took five roebuck and four medal-class boar in a short time. I saw huge stags everywhere we ventured. I had to return. I made plans with Dr. Ion Vava and Toni to hunt red deer during the rut and follow up with boar, roebuck, and fallow deer.

In mid-September, Dr. Marinos Petratos, Toni, and I flew into Romania. First, we hunted stag around the Pischia area between Arad and Timisoara. The woods were packed with game after seventeen years of only Ceauşescu shooting the big stuff. Animals roamed all day long. You could hunt anytime your little heart desired. The first morning, as the sun was rising, Marinos's rifle shot split the air. He had quickly connected on a medal-class stag. Red deer appeared everywhere unfazed, whether we stalked through the forest or sat in stands. Stag, boar, fallow deer, and roebuck roamed in broad daylight. We were the first outsiders allowed in this area in many years. We felt like nobles of old, afoot in pristine forests filled with trophy-quality game. This former preserve was evidence of what European hunters could do if given enough time.

I pushed a dozen or so stags the first three days and took a medal-class boar on one stalk. On the fourth day, I was guiding Marinos to his stand when we heard heavy feet crackling the branches of thick bushes. I motioned to Marinos to freeze. We were right off the tree line, just outside the field. An old bull barely came into view, but I was able to get a glimpse of the top of a pair of black antlers. I knew he was an old stag by the color and thickness of the antlers. The old boy moved cautiously into the open field. His smoky breath was rising as he let out mellow roars. He was big-bodied with a thick neck. I surmised him to be nine or ten years old with a rack of more than nine kilos. As he turned his head, the old bull spotted me. He had the deer in the headlights look implying, "Oh, no!" I squeezed the trigger. My gun was up and ready as soon as I saw his antlers. The stag fell hard where he had left the woods. The silver-medal stag was mine. Now, Marinos and I both had a stag and a boar, but neither a fallow deer nor a roebuck.

We went to Sarlota, which is a bit farther north. We took four trophy fallow bucks in two days of hunting. We had seen hundreds. We moved to Banloc for roebuck. Toni's old friend Emil Nadra, the head hunter for the area, had a problem—too many roebuck. The area had been a royal hunting ground of Queen Maria of Romania and roebuck were everywhere. In just three days, we saw one hundred and fifty to two hundred bucks. Marinos connected on a huge gold-medal deer the afternoon of the second day, which brought our total to seven in just forty-eight hours.

A stag roars his presence to all comers. Illustration by Zoltan Boros

On our last day in this prime area, we decided Marinos would head out for another roebuck without me, and I would accompany Nadra. We were searching for a good roebuck field when the doctor's car suddenly stopped. As we exited the vehicle to examine the problem, an old stag roared. The doctor knew the forests well—as well as the animals that lived and moved through the area. He was sure there were no known big stags in the immediate region. Being ever so curious, I suggested we have a look anyway. We hiked into the darkened thick forest, moving at a snail's pace to not be heard. We saw the old king minding his own business, and we plotted a way to move around him. This is an easy decision when you know you are just looking. We inched our way to within one hundred yards, then fifty, and I froze. I squinted to try to get a better look through the trees and fading light obscured by the clouds. I could see the stag's body, but his antlers were hidden behind thick branches. I raised my binoculars for a better look and discovered that the branches I had been staring at were actually the old boy's antlers. Or, I should say with a bit more accuracy, it was the stag's left antler. They were as big as any I had seen in the hunting museum in Budapest. I knew the deer was large, maybe record-book large. Nadra was uttering the stag was ten, then eleven kilos. "The museum's stags seemed smaller," I thought. It couldn't be, or could it?

Just then, as often happens, the brute dashed to the end of the forest and into a freshly plowed field. "There he goes," I sadly sputtered to Nadra. But we kept still and quiet. A few moments later, a roebuck barked and the old stag stopped to see what all the fuss was about. Luckily, we had already made it to the tree line, and I had positioned my gun on a branch just in case something like this might occur. As the old guy turned back, I whispered, "Bad move." I knew Diana the Huntress was about to give me one of her most prized possessions. I was almost in a trance as I squeezed the trigger.

We hurried into the field. Dr. Nadra said he thought the stag's antlers were eleven kilos, but the antlers kept getting bigger and bigger as we got closer. Standing approximately twenty yards from this fallen king of the forest, my legs almost went out from under me. I had not experienced that exuberant feeling since my first cape buffalo in Kenya. "God, what a monster!" I panted in a low voice to Dr. Nadra. I was certain I had a special trophy.

Marinos and myself with our crew and the monster of Banloc.

Six guides came from the lodge with a tractor and trailer. Marinos, Dr. Nadra, and I led the way in our four-wheel-drive truck. Marinos, never at a loss for words, was speechless as we approached the stag and remained so until after the half-dozen men struggled to get our prize onto the back of the trailer. We took pictures, said our goodbyes, and headed back to Pischia, where we met Toni, who was already setting up groups for me to bring to the area next year. In those days, you only had little East German cars to carry the game. The stag antlers completely covered the top of our small red car.

As we drove up to the lodge, Toni was standing in the driveway with two guides. He had been told about the monster stag I had taken. They had not had many hunters in many years, so no one really knew how big the stag would actually score. As Toni caught a glimpse of the dangling antlers, he began yelling and jumping up and down—all this from my friend who is usually rather subdued. Toni kept screaming, "What did you do?! What did you do?!" He was so animated that I was afraid I had shot the Romanian version of Bambi, and Toni began repeating that this was the biggest stag he had ever seen. The next day, the official scoring committee from Timisoara examined my trophy, as did hunters from surrounding areas. The antlers weighed 15.6 kilos and scored more than 260 CIC points—one of biggest wild stags ever

Here, I'm still in shock several hours after taking the stag of a lifetime.

taken. As a matter of fact, the old boy would have been a near world record until 1971. Toni was right. The stags of Eastern Europe truly were the giant cousins of stags in Spain and Scotland.

The high stayed with me for days. I was interviewed for Romanian television and several newspaper articles were written about our hunt. The stag is now on display in the Beretta Gallery in New York City.

Chapter Four

Wolf by Transylvanian Moonlight

———

Toni has a longtime friend, Cornel, who is the head hunter of the Criva area of Romania. The Criva region is known for bear, boar, and wolf (*Canis lupus*). Cornel was kind enough to arrange an impromptu driven hunt for Toni and me. We slept for three days in a sheepherder's shed and produced eleven nice boar and three foxes. We now had four or five days left to attempt other types of game. Roaming the area were stag, roebuck, wild boar, chamois, and, oh yes, the wolf. It seems a pack of wolves had been killing sheep not five miles from where we were staying. With that in mind, we drove into the mountains for a good hour or so and walked for the next two hours to what I thought would be a mighty cold night spent sleeping in an open blind so we could look for signs of the wolf pack. The "blind," as it turned out, was actually a small house built thirty feet up in some strong trees. Inside, we found a heater, bathroom, and two beds that overlooked a spot where an old horse breathed his last to save the townsfolk's livestock.

The temperature dropped below zero. The moon was full. We were in Transylvania hunting wolves. Snow was on the ground. When the moonlight hit the snow, it illuminated the meadow as if it were the afternoon. We cracked open the windows, watching and listening for the crunch of wolf paws on the crisp snow or some pronounced howling. We felt like we were in an old Lon Chaney movie. My guide and I took turns observing,

A wolf of the Carpathian Mountains. Illustration by Zoltan Boros

drinking strong tea, and sleeping. Just as I was peering out the window around 1:30 a.m., a sound came out of the night that always makes one's blood run cold. It was the eerie howling of a wolf. As I scoped the field to my left about five hundred yards out, I noticed one, then two, then five wolves slowly approaching the blind. Quickly, I nudged the guide and pointed with great vigor. We watched as the pack closed in at four hundred yards, two hundred yards, one hundred and fifty yards, and then they disappeared the same way they had appeared, as if by magic.

Had the pack seen or heard my rifle rise up? It couldn't have been. I have made that silent move hundreds of times on everything from turkeys to elephants and never lost one for that reason. Well, I guess there is always a first time. We closed the window and began feeling quite sorry for ourselves. After a two-hour nap, it was again my turn to be lookout. Through tired eyes, I stared at the spot where the pack had last been standing and tried to figure out which direction they ran. Through the trees? Into a ravine? I skimmed the area focusing intently on the snow. Then, I saw them! There were footprints not too far from where the wolves had disappeared. I noticed that one set of tracks was heading toward the bait. I quickly glanced in that direction and there, having a late night snack, was a huge black wolf. There was no time to waste using binoculars. I woke the guide, raised the window, slid my .30-06 out the opening, and immediately found the target in the moonlit, snow-covered field. I squeezed the trigger, and he fell to the ground. Unexpectedly, the beast jumped up and began biting at his wound—just like an African lion—and staggered toward the woods. By this time, another 180-grain Federal was in the pipe.

Joining the canine family, along with the mighty wolf and crafty fox, is the golden jackal.

I hammered him again; no one wants to search for a wounded wolf in the dark. He never moved after the second crack of the .30-06 echoed off the mountaintops. We waited fifteen minutes or so before descending the ladder. With my rifle and the guide's shotgun at the ready, we moved up on the wolf from the rear, as those bad boys have been known to play possum. He was stone dead, with two neatly placed (if I may say so) shots in the kill zone. We were now jumping up and down for joy at 3:45 a.m.! After dressing the beast, we hung him up on the side of the blind to keep him from becoming someone else's dinner. We slept until the sun came up around 6:30 a.m. and headed down the mountain to fetch a horse and sleigh to haul out our trophy.

As it turned out, the wolf was a big male that had ventured away from the pack for his late-night snack. Over the next three months, hunters bagged two more of these dangerous sheep killers.

A high-mountain dweller.

A big party was thrown in my honor for ridding the area of this fearful menace. We dined on roasted meat, potatoes, three kinds of salad, and way too much Palinca, the local apple moonshine, which is considered a brandy. My advice is to stay away from this firewater. Let's just say I could taste it for the next two days with an all-too-constant regularity.

The wolf is a trophy that is usually found by being in the right place at the right time, rather than as a specific animal you come to hunt. I have seen wolves only twice on my many trips to the Carpathian Mountains of Romania. It is this animal's uncanny ability to avoid his archenemy—man—that has kept him howling since the earliest hunter came to fear that bloodcurdling sound. After listening to the music of this beast from Spain to Montana, I can tell you that anytime you hear the howl, it awakens some primordial emotion and reflex. Perhaps it is a memory from long ago when we first hunted the wolf, or he hunted us.

Chapter Five

Driven Pheasant at Abadszalok

The quality of driven pheasant shooting in Hungary is often compared to the traditional shoots of England and Scotland. It is a subject of great debate. As someone who has been on a good number of shoots in both areas and Ireland, I will attempt to set the record straight. The British Isles have no equal for the way Americans are brought up to think about driven pheasant shooting. The forests are beautiful. The lawns are manicured. The manor houses are fit for kings. Tweed-clad gamekeepers and mud-covered Range Rovers complete the image of a proper English pheasant shoot.

The birds in England are no longer wild. They are released in April and the survivors are fairly wild by the time the shoots occur in

One heck of a drive.

November, December, and January. In Britain today, 0 to 5 percent of the birds are wild. In most of Hungary, it is down to 10 or 20 percent. Those are not the only differences.

In England, birds are usually driven from hills or forests with the guns waiting beyond tall trees. In Hungary, with its flat land, birds are often driven from cornfields toward small forests with guns stationed along the first line of trees. There is always talk about the birds flying low in Hungary, and this is true compared to Britain's hills, but it happens for two principle reasons that are not often fully understood: the lay of the land and the number of wild birds. Why shoot at a low bird when there may be five or six hundred birds flying over the line in a single drive? The number of birds on a top Hungarian pheasant shoot far exceeds the birds available during a shoot in England or Scotland. In Hungary, I have learned to take only sporting birds. You can pick and choose your shot on almost every drive. There have been times when I never fired a single shot on a stand in England. I have ended such days feeling I paid top dollar to stand amongst a pastoral scene (worthy of the canvas of some great master whose work hangs in museums) when I wanted to participate in a world-class shoot with plenty of trigger action.

The cost of a shoot in Britain is often 50 to 60 percent higher than the price of a similar shoot in Hungary. Once you have paid the continually rising prices of Britain, Hungary seems like a real bargain. Today, Abadszalok is one of the most expensive places in Hungary to shoot, but back in the mid-1980s, it was undiscovered by Americans and most of the rest of Europe. Hungarian bird hunting has its own unique flavor and tradition. I do like the tradition of England but for

a different kind of shooting. My heart is now in Hungary, a place we first came to know when it was still under communist rule. I don't remember how exactly we got the idea to hunt in Hungary, but we were on a driven shoot at Peter Salms's estate, Port of Missing Men—so named because men would escape the cares of the

There's nothing like some good hot soup after several storybook drives.

world at this magnificent property on the shores of the Peconic Bay on Eastern Long Island. It was here that Bruno and Veronique Bich, Bill Hooks, Buzz Allen, Prince Anton Windisch-Gratz, Tom Ruger, Debbie, and I suddenly decided to go on a shoot in Hungary. We had all heard the stories that were just starting to spread through the international hunting community about the quality of the birds and hunts. Besides, we wanted to see Budapest.

When we arrived, Russians were everywhere. We stayed at the Hilton on Castle Hill on the Buda side of the city. I used to love to stay there before moving over to the Le Meridion Hotel on the more convenient Pest side of the Danube. It had an incredible view of the Danube from the old section of the city, laced with many quaint walking streets. Whenever possible, I like our hunting groups to stay at least a full day in Budapest to see the Paris of the East. She may seem a bit tired after almost forty years of oppressive communist rule, but she is a vibrant, beautiful city that should be on the must-see list of world travelers. Once, Budapest was part of the Austro-Hungarian Empire, and her many grand buildings, bridges, and squares attest to her former glory. Besides, just two hours beyond the edge of the city is Abadszalok. Between the city and Abadszalok are hundreds and hundreds of plowed fields planted in rye, kale, and corn.

Our hunting area was just outside Abadszalok's town limits. We stayed in a place that was definitely not built as a hunting residence for some bygone noble—it was a working hunting lodge. The main building had offices, a large dining room, and a full kitchen. The sleeping rooms were in two other buildings a short walk away. The quarters were small and not everyone had a private bathroom. This was a far cry from the small hotels and former Barons' homes we found in later years. It was rough by British standards, to say the least, but what we experienced in the fields around that modest lodge over the next four days more than made up for the housing. I remember it like it was yesterday, and I often revisit the shoot in my mind.

It was late November. The ground was covered with frost when we ventured out the first morning. The wind was steady and just above the freezing point. The sun settled behind a blanket of clouds. It was a perfect day for a pheasant shoot. We discussed the rules and etiquette of the field and drew for stands. Mine was lucky number seven, which is usually one of the average positions for a great shoot. Toni stood directly behind me, alongside my loader, Istvan. Soon after the bugle sounded and the shoot began, a wild, colorful thing with a tail about a foot and a half long burst into the air. He crossed somewhere down the line and Bruno cracked him. Suddenly, we began to hear the left line of beaters working the birds into the middle of the trees. There were about a hundred beaters working the woods, divided into sections.

I just love the dogs.

We had twenty-five on the left, twenty-five on the right, and fifty or so down the center.

Toni put his hand on my shoulder, leaned in close to my ear, and quietly warned that a fox may appear from the left. Oftentimes you can hear the pheasants squawking or see them jumping in the air when a fox, cat, dog, or weasel tries moving away from the beaters. As there were no pheasants in the air, we watched the area and hoped a fox would rush for mad escape. Sure enough, a large red fox shot from behind the trees with no beaters for four hundred yards. I let loose with two number fives, and Debbie now had her first Hungarian fox hat.

In the next ten minutes, we watched two, then four, then ten pheasant stream into the field from the woods just in front of us. Suddenly, we saw one hundred, then two hundred, then twenty, then fifty come whizzing by. It was that way for the next thirty minutes. We were participating in the perfect drive, which one often hears about and always hopes to be lucky enough to experience.

When the end of the drive was signaled by the sound of the hunting horn, not one of us could believe what we had seen and done. There were as many pheasants—good, fast, and high birds—on the ground as one would see in an entire day in England. Perhaps seven to eight hundred had passed over the guns, not to mention all the birds that flew back over the beaters or escaped out the sides.

The end of a perfect hunt—the type that stays fresh in your shooting memories forever.

Everyone was in a state of shock. Buzz, Bruno, and I had seen some big drives, but this was the mother lode. Buzz turned to me and stated with great zeal, "No matter what happens the rest of the shoot, you have shown me more than I ever anticipated." The new guns had an idea of what to expect, but until you see the sky covered with pheasants, you have no way of knowing the permanent effect it has on your sporting memory.

I remember complaining to Toni that the shooting was so good that we would have no pheasants left for the next three days. He chuckled. "There are sixty or seventy thousand birds about, spread over endless forests and cornfields, so I don't think you need to worry," Toni said.

Everyone was in awe during the presentation of the birds. We had just finished the perfect day with five drives and everyone shot well at each stand. The birds had been arranged ten in a row with cocks on one side and hens on the other. Six foxes and three ducks added to the total count. I will not put the bag number down, as future generations may not believe what they read, but suffice it to say that it was the equivalent of three days of shooting in Great Britain. It was a shoot that Sir Joe Nickerson and the Prince of Wales would have given a silver plaque to commemorate, to say the least.

To have a truly great shoot, you have to have a good number of dedicated hunters.

The spirit of the day continued into dinner. We toasted the fine birds and joked about our misses, but even the beginners knew they had witnessed shooting as fine and pristine as what the nobility experienced before the Great War.

I have had the honor to shoot driven grouse in England and Scotland and driven partridge in Spain on some of its finest estates. Each bird brings back exciting memories of fabulous shoots. My greatest remembrances do not always have to do with the bag but with the quality of the birds and companionship of the line. To this day, a one hundred and seventy-five pheasant bag in Kent was one of my most impressive experiences, as it was my first test with driven birds, yet this first Hungarian shoot in Abadszalok stands out most vividly in my recollections of great driven adventures.

The next three days of the shoot were the same as the first. We took a much-needed day off in the middle of the four days. Some of the guys just rested, some went sightseeing, and some—my group—went antiquing. The problem with shopping with a couple friends such as Bruno and Buzz is that we all like the same old treasures. After Bruno bought a painting that Buzz and I also admired (he was the first person through the door and spotted it straight away), I knew I needed a plan

Our good family friend Dr. John Shane, whom I forgive for using his fine pair of Hollands.

for the next stop. So before the car even came to a halt, I jumped out and had my hands on a French bronze of St. Hubertus, the patron saint of hunters, before either of the other two treasure hunters put their feet on the pavement.

After four days of first-rate shooting, the group was ready to head back to Budapest, where we were to meet up with one of my other arriving shoots. Believe me, we had plenty of stories to tell to get these boys champing at the bit. From that first shoot, we expanded to as many as seven hunts per season—any more than this, and the quality can suffer. There are many places in Hungary to shoot driven birds, but after twenty-five or so years, we think we have the right ones.

In later years, we discovered flighted ducks in Hungary could be added to our driven pheasant days. Shooting waterfowl with full and extra-full chokes from stands in and around lakes proved to be a welcome addition. Two days of driven pheasant, two days of flighted ducks, and a day of walkups for wild pheasant and hare thrown in the middle will cure your lust for bird shooting for quite some time.

Chapter Six

The Stags of Lake Balaton

In September of 1989, I was drawn back to Hungary to search for stag. This time, I would hunt the Zala region in the forests and hills near the Austrian border, within the foothills of the Alps. The trip was special to me. I was joined by my friend Steven Weiss, with whom I had hunted since 1969, when we traveled to Surinam looking for jaguar. We have since shared many sporting adventures from Kenya to Zimbabwe and Spain to Romania. Now, we were once again airborne and on our way to some distant land in the midst of a well-worn ritual.

We were flying to Budapest, where we would embark in search of some of Europe's biggest red deer. Luckily, the flight from New York to

You'll find vineyard after vineyard all around Lake Balaton.

Hungary is direct, which was a big improvement from when we first traveled to Surinam. I have spent so much time traveling in pursuit of game that I have it down pretty well: two meals, two movies, three hours of sleep, no alcohol, some good hunting magazines, and—voila—you are on the ground and moving around. Yet no matter how often I make these trips, I am never fully relaxed until all my bags are back in my possession. I have the same concern on each trip and the same silent refrain always sounds in my head: "Will my rifle arrive? Will my suitcase and duffle show up on the conveyor belt?" I have learned to pack my hunting gear equally in separate bags to even the luggage loss playing field.

All four bags soon showed up along with Steven's gun case. As we waited for the last bag to be loaded onto the conveyor belt, my gun case was nowhere to be found. We checked the oversized areas and asked the local baggage handlers, and there was still nothing but that bad feeling and a visit to the lost and found baggage counter. The agent had good news and bad news. The airline found the case—in West Palm Beach, Florida. Delta helpfully routed the rifle so it would arrive on the same flight we came in on the next morning. Steven and I headed to Budapest and spent the lost day sightseeing. But always in the back of my mind was the reverberating concern—will the rifle really arrive as promised?

The rifle indeed arrived on time and we rushed headlong to Zala; we were two old friends hoping for another perfect hunt in a country far from home. We arrived at the lodge only to discover that our rooms had been given away to two German hunters because we did not come in the day before as planned. Toni, my partner, took care of everything. He knows everyone to know in Hungary and Romania, and he counted the head hunter of Zala amongst his close friends. As luck would have it—and it was luck—a new hunting lodge was under construction in the middle of an area famous for world-class stag. The lodge was 90 percent complete and no hunters were due to arrive until the following year, but nothing was going to be easy on this trip.

On our first hunt, the skies opened, and rain poured down as we made our way through thousands of acres of forest and huge fields that stretched as far as the eye could see. I muttered softly to myself, "What next?" But soon the heavy rains stopped, and I hoped all the animals in the forest, which hopefully included huge stag, would be moving about trying to get dry. The temperature was dropping, too, which was another plus to help the game start moving. My guide suggested waiting until early the next morning, to which I quickly responded that we had already lost a day and should find a good stand where a few stags might appear.

We nestled into a high blind in a tree that overlooked a vast field. At any time or any place, a mighty stag might appear. It was cloudy. A

While we sat in a morning blind, a stag appeared as if by magic.

chill hung in the air. The wind was slight. The weather was cooperating. But where were the red deer? Off to the left, we spotted three roebucks grazing. After a short while, a hind and some hare visited our field for dinner. Then, a young stag nervously stepped out of the forest following a hind. They stayed only a short time. I thought this was probably a good omen. The youngster may have been trying to keep his distance from the big boy who owned that piece of terra firma. Soon the sky darkened, and a large shadow moved over the field and absorbed the light. This made spotting game difficult. I was thinking of how nice it would be to sit by a warm fire in the lodge sipping coffee. But I had one of my feelings, so we were wet and cold in a tree stand watching a darkening field.

Suddenly, I caught a glimpse of an outline of something walking in the darkness just inside the shadow of the night. Through Steiner binoculars, I could make out three hinds and a large stag. I signaled my guide. He glassed the animal and tried to quickly judge the antlers and age of the noble beast. As he contemplated the answers, the light was losing out to the quickly approaching darkness. In a moment of serendipity, the stag turned into the light. He was an old boy with twelve points. My safety was off. I had my shot planned. I had already seen the stag's antlers and body in the split second before the guide could raise his binoculars, and I squeezed the trigger as the guide was muttering the "O" in "OK." I knew night would protect the stag in just a few moments.

After a lost rifle, no room in the lodge, and cold September rain, a high silver-medal stag was on the ground. My hunt was over, and I had four days to help scout a good stag for Steven.

The weather turned fair as quickly as my luck had that first night. Cool mornings and evenings were divided by perfect afternoons. I saw

This beauty was taken just as the night was swallowing up the last rays of the day.

a couple of smoker stags the next several days, but I was only looking with Toni. One was a gold-medal with at least fourteen points that we caught crossing a dirt road on his way back to seclusion. Another disappeared into a deep forest, but not before showing us his massive rack. We never saw either of them again. We could have easily taken a half-dozen mature stags. The rut was in full swing.

During our scouting treks, we constantly saw wild boar tracks in the mud. Some tracks were made by real bruisers. I managed to get the guide to tell me about a super wallow deep within the woods that was a favorite boar haunt. The first night, we picked a spot with several bushes and trees that made a natural blind. Several sows with small boar were our only reward. The next night we brought blankets and food—we were ready for the long haul. About 10:30 p.m., a big-bodied boar came out and then another. I could not make out tusks on either, but I did manage to see a hump on the bigger one. As this wasn't a trophy hunt, I let go, and the boar fell straight down. The second one had no idea where we were, so it came right for us. Two quick rounds and I had a couple of nice boar to add to the luck train for the week. As we slowly approached the bigger one, I estimated the tusks measured at more than nineteen centimeters. It was a nice wall hanger, and the second one turned out to be a fat old sow. Boar was the main course for the following evening.

It was now the last night, and we sat quietly waiting for Mr. Weiss to return with news. As the agent at Delta said about my gun, Steven had good news and bad news. The good news was that he had taken what he thought to be a good shot on a nice stag. However, when they followed the blood trail into the forest, the old boy was nowhere to be seen. Steven started doubting the shot, as I have many times. Maybe it was a bit high? Perhaps it was too low or too far back? I have spent many sleepless nights, as Steven did, over these questions.

We headed out at first light on our last morning with extra guides to look for Mr. Stag. We must have been searching for four hours when a young boy appeared and asked if we had shot a stag the night before. Everyone was immediately interested in his question. It seems his father had almost run over a dead deer in a field he was plowing with his trac- tor. The medal-class stag was a half-mile from where it was shot. I asked Steven where his shot landed on the deer and his answer was on the left side around the lungs. We then turned the beast over to his left side and discovered the shot at the top of the lungs. It never ceases to amaze me how far some animals travel after what should have been a kill shot. As hunters, we all want to see the animal fall immediately after a well-placed shot, but what happens once the bullet enters the animal, the angle of entry, or a deflection from bone are factors often beyond control.

I knew Steven was happier than anyone in the group, as his sleepless night turned into a day of jubilation. The drive back to Budapest was filled with jokes and light-hearted conversation. We talked of many new adven- tures from fallow deer in Hungary to chamois in Romania. As it is with most trips, before one ends you are dreaming of the next.

Brother Harry Hersey with the second largest stag we ever took. The antlers weighed 14.38 kilograms.

Chapter Seven

Twenty Years in Search of the Monster Roebuck of Hungary

———

The roebuck, crafty and elusive, inspires a near fanaticism among Europe's big-game hunters, much as the whitetail deer intrigues so many American riflemen. Hunters in Germany, Austria, Italy, France, and Spain closely follow the roebuck season. The small buck is so fast and wily that it challenges even the most skilled hunters. In short, roebuck hunting is addictive. A dedicated European sportsman often hunts one hundred to three hundred bucks in a lifetime. My introduction to roebuck came in the late 1970s in Spain and Great Britain. Then, roebucks were typically afterthoughts at the end of stag or boar hunts as an extra bonus.

In those days, the small deer held no special interest for me. I was after their bigger cousins. But by 1985, while stalking red stag in the pristine forests of the Zemplen Mountains, I discovered a new appreciation for roebuck when I crossed paths with one that exhibited bigger antlers than I had ever seen in Spain or Great Britain. Later that day, during dinner with my hunting partner of twenty-five years, Angiolo Bellini; his wife, Elizabetta; and my wife, Debbie, I casually mentioned what I had seen in the forest. Angiolo, who has introduced me to so much in so many different places, laughed.

Hungary's Great Plain: prime roebuck territory.

"You are in the land of the best roebuck found in all of Europe!" Angiolo said. He was not exaggerating. Little did I know, several world-record roebucks had been taken within a two-hour drive of our hunting lodge. Every year, these areas around Puszta, or Hungary's Great Plain, yield many of Europe's largest gold-medal roebucks. Such knowledge has long been quietly known to seasoned European hunters, such as Angiolo. So by dinner's end, we had decided to forgo red stag, albeit temporarily, and drive down the mountain toward Debrecen, an area famous for roebuck. We stopped, as is our custom, at hunting lodges along the way to see the beauties that had roamed the fields and forests of Debrecen. We saw recently collected trophies neatly lining the walls. Now I, having spent a life in pursuit of big game, started feeling I had missed something great as we stood and studied the height and thickness of the many different-shaped sets of antlers arrayed on these hunting lodge walls.

I soon realized I was in the equivalent of a whitetail area that contained all 130- to 200-inch examples of *Odocoileus virginianus*, a feeling that would soon be proven by the area's head hunter, Marozsan Karoly, who was to become my guide on many future hunts. Over lunch, he showed us pictures of even bigger bucks taken during the first two weeks of the season. A quick drive around small portion of the twenty-thousand-acre hunting area showed roebuck everywhere. They were in the forests and along endless hedgerows that surrounded field after field. I had seen enough. I felt the spirit of the roebuck that lures so many European hunters back and back again.

Yet the Hungarian roebuck has always existed behind Hungary's own Iron Curtain. I am convinced some hunters spread rumors that Hungary was a difficult place to hunt, so they could keep Hungary to themselves. It was an easy rumor to spread. At the time, the communists and Russians were in charge of the country, and it was difficult to get international hunters to hunt Hungary. Of course, the rumors were absolutely untrue. Even under communist rule, Hungary welcomed sportsmen—that's how strong the hunting culture is, was, and will remain. Now, as it was then, your gun permit is issued upon arrival at Hungarian customs. Hunting licenses are completed before entering the country. A sportsman is welcomed everywhere, especially in and around the hunting areas. Hunting is woven into the traditions of the Hungarian countryside. The roebuck occupies a special niche in this tradition. Until the mid-eighties, roebuck season started on May 1, though it has since been rolled back to April 15—before the crops and foliage are so high and dense that they easily hide this forty- to sixty-pound trophy. We have spent good times in pursuit of the roebuck over the years. I remember on one hunt Angiolo, Dr. Marinos Petratos, and I managed two gold, two silver, and four bronze CIC medal-class animals out of the twenty-four deer taken from an area not known to produce good bucks.

For an animal admired by so many European hunters, the rise of the roebuck is a surprisingly recent phenomenon compared to the long traditions of the continent's other game animals.

During the Middle Ages, roe deer were not as important as other big game—such as the European bison, red stag, or brown bear—nor were they mentioned much in any of the books of that time as significant game animals. The roebuck decisively entered hunting literature around the seventeenth and eighteenth centuries when most of the bear, wolf, lynx, and boar had been hunted. There is something poetic about roe deer, or *Capreolus capreolus*—the formal name assigned to roe deer in 1758 by Carl Linnaeus, the great Swedish physician and zoologist who developed the system we use today for naming animals and organisms. The European Roebuck, the smallest native of Europe's Cervidae family, lives over almost the entire European continent. They are also found in Little Asia, the Caucasus Mountains, and on the southern side of the Caspian Sea that borders Iran. In Europe, the density of the roebuck population differs from region to region. The highest number of roebucks seems to live in Germany, Austria, Hungary, Poland, Czechoslovakia, Slovakia, Romania, Serbia, and Croatia. Smaller populations live in Portugal, Holland, and Finland. Some are also found in the forests of Scotland, Sweden, in the Alps of Switzerland, and Russia. In Hungary, the oldest roebuck antlers ever found date from the Neolithic period.

After World War II, agricultural methods changed considerably with mechanization, and collectives helped Europe's roebuck population explode—especially in Hungary, Romania, Czechoslovakia, Poland, Yugoslavia, and parts of the Soviet Union and Bulgaria. Suddenly, roebuck began appearing on plains where only hares and birds were hunted. There were much more abundant food sources than they had found in the forest. Soon, the antlers and bodies of the roebuck grew larger, and a European hunting tradition was born. Of course, the small male deer is called a buck, the female a doe, and deer younger than a year old are fawns. Only the bucks have antlers, which they lose in late autumn or early winter and are grown once again in the spring. The roebuck body is completely developed by his second year. The height of a mature buck in Central Europe is 70 to 82 centimeters, or 27 ½ to 32 inches.

The average body length is 114.8 centimeters, or about 45 inches.

In front of the hotel Hodi, from left to right: Chris Wyatt, Bill Hooks, Bill Schaefer, Peter Horn, Steven Weiss, and Alan Romney.

Females are 67 to 72 centimeters, or 26 to 28 inches, with a length of 112.8 cm, or 44 inches. The average weight of a buck is about 40 to 60 pounds, and a doe is 40 to 50 pounds. The size and weight will vary from area to area, especially with reference to food and mineral supply. Hunting roebucks for trophies is a popular tradition in Europe, particularly in Germany and the old territory of the Austrian-Hungarian Empire. However, excellent trophies were recently shot in England, Sweden, and now in Italy, Spain, and France. In countries with a strong tradition of trophy hunting, bucks are taken with rifles by waiting in stands or stalking. In France and Belgium, they are shot on driven hunts, mostly with shotguns, and even in the late fall and winter when they have shed their antlers.

The main seasons for roebuck hunting in Central Europe are in spring, specifically April and May—when the vegetation is not too high and the hunters can identify the bucks they want to shoot—and in the summer, from the end of July through the first half of August—when you can call the bucks in during the rut.

The highest number of roebucks with capital trophies is taken in Hungary. This is due to a combination of incredible genetic characteristics and the constant work of highly qualified professional hunters who tend and nurture the herds. The roebuck trophies are classified accordingly to the CIC formula. Bronze medals are between 105 and 114.99 points, silver medals between 115 and 129.99 points, and gold medals are anything more than 130 points.

The best Hungarian roebuck population lives in the regions of Jász-Nagykun-Szolnok, Szabolcs-Szatmár-Bereg, Békés, Hajdú-Bihar, and most of Eastern Hungary. Almost any country where roebuck are found occasionally produces a monster head. Romania, Sweden, and England often generate first-class trophies.

Roebucks are first measured by the weight of their antlers and a predetermined part of the skull mass. A good head weighs from 325 to 350 grams. Approximately 390 grams equals a bronze medal, 420 grams a silver, and 500 grams signifies a gold medal. There are, of course, many other factors that determine the CIC medal class, such as length, mass, number of points, symmetry, color, and the overall beauty of

Chris Wyatt with his first roebuck of the hunt—758 grams.

the trophy. Over the years, our clients have taken many notable heads. In 2003, Chris Wyatt bagged a 758-gram roebuck that was the heaviest trophy in Hungary that year. In 2011, Roger Carter turned in a buck that weighed 758 grams—yes, the exact same weight as Chris Wyatt's—along with three others weighing more than 600 grams. He also managed to score the magical perruque, a buck with massive velvet-like antlers. My wife Debbie recently shot a 675-gram monster on the same hunt where I managed a 603-gram trophy. Pamela and Stan Atwood took roebucks of 654 and 634 grams, respectfully.

Our sportsmen have taken eleven bucks of more than 700 grams and 88 of more than 600 grams. We have had many groups with truly amazing results, such as Alain Boucheron and friends, who took eleven gold medals in a single week. Steven Weiss, a hunting partner of mine for more than forty years, took all medal-class roebuck, which consisted of two gold, three silver, and three bronze medals in a week during 2005, one of the best roebuck years. It was on the same hunt that our good friend William Grey Schaefer, "Uncle Billie," managed two gold, three silver, and two bronze medals. I remember that opening week as if it were yesterday. Our hunters totaled 47 CIC medal roebucks out of 61 taken, and all of them were SCI book class.

The World's Best Roebuck (*SCI Edition Seven*)

Out of the top ten roebuck listed below, six are from Hungary and one is from Romania.

Location	Score
Hungary, Szoreg	58 $\frac{5}{8}$
Spain, Urbion Mts.	58 $\frac{3}{8}$
Poland, Krakow	57 $\frac{2}{8}$
Romania	56 $\frac{6}{8}$
Hungary, Szoreg	56 $\frac{4}{8}$
Hungary, Bataapati	56 $\frac{4}{8}$
Hungary, Szoreg	56 $\frac{2}{8}$
Hungary, Szentes	56
Sweden, Vanersborg	55 $\frac{6}{8}$
Hungary, Szolnok	55 $\frac{3}{8}$

Know Your Rifle

The question always arises as to what rifle is best suited for *Capreolus capreolus*. I ultimately choose my rifle based on other animals I will be hunting, such as stag, wild boar, fallow, and so forth. I have long used my favorite Paul Jaeger .270 to make shots from eighty to three hundred yards, and I have also employed a broad battery of Sako & Tikka rifles ranging from the fast and flat .22-250 to the hard-hitting .300 WSM. The 6.5x55, .243, 7x57, .270 WSM, .280 Remington, .30-06, and .300 WSM have never failed me. Light calibers, such as the .22-250 and .243, are superb for long-range shots in open areas but not ideal for tangled thickets. The .300 WSM may be a bit much, but it will anchor a buck at more than four hundred yards. What matters, especially when shooting long distances, is that you practice with your rifle and are familiar with your weapon.

Before any hunt, it is wise to get a small deer target and practice, practice, practice. Shoot at two hundred, three hundred, and four hundred yards, so you know exactly what your rifle will do and, more importantly, what it will not do. Remember to shoot only as far as you are personally comfortable. I make sure my rifle is sighted in by practicing on my hunting property in Duchess County, New York

Antal "Toni" Török (left) with a monster perruque or wig buck.

that I own with Don Trump Jr. One of the fields has a five-hundred-yard range thanks to Eric Trump, who put it together. By shooting from all positions, whether from a shooting stick, tree, or rock, I am prepared for any field scenario. You will encounter hunting conditions of great diversity.

I have hunted roebuck everywhere in Hungary. I have hunted in the mountains by Lake Balaton and on all the borders of Hungary's seven neighbors. I know the best areas that always seem to produce the finest trophies. I also know the areas that are famous for introducing hunters to Hungarian, and even Romanian, hunting. Once you have experienced the hunt, whether in a vineyard or a field of wheat, I think you will find that the wily little roebuck somehow manages to make you return just one more time. Each year I say I will pass opening week, and each year the little bucks of Puszta beckon me once again.

An Additional View of Hunting Roebuck in Hungary by Steven Weiss

The roebuck, *Capreolus capreolus*, is one of the oldest and most traditional European hunting trophies. The finest trophies are in Eastern Hungary, so I was thrilled when my old friend and hunting companion Peter Horn asked me to join him and some other friends for a reunion hunt in a prime area.

Mid-April found me in Nyirbator, a little town some twenty kilometers from Hungary's Eastern border with Romania, with Peter, Bill Schaefer, Chris Wyatt, Alan Romney, and Bill Hooks. This area is primarily farmland with vast acres of fields and stands of beautifully maintained forests. The quantity and quality of animals are incredible. It was not unusual to glass sixty to eighty animals per day. Good binoculars are a must!

Although the roebuck is a smaller member of the deer family, weighing 40 to 60 pounds, they are fast and wary. A good light, flat shooting rifle is a necessity, as shots are quick and often in the range of 200 or more meters. Anything ranging from a minimum of the .22-250 up to the many .30 calibers will suffice. I was using a brand new Tikka T-3 short-action in .300WSM with a Burris 3x9 scope. My 150-grain bullets produced a one-shot kill every time with the animals rarely moving more than a few feet. Our group success was staggering. We had a total of eight gold medals. The guides, accommodations, and logistics were all first-rate thanks to Peter's partner, Toni Török, and Pannonvad of Budapest. To enjoy this caliber of hunting in the world today is extraordinary, and it is all more special to share it with old friends.

A happy Alain Boucheron with a nice old buck.

Chapter Eight

Driven Wild Boar Below Lake Balaton: The Case of the Flying Hind

A hunting lodge is more than a place to rest. Seasoned hunters know hunting lodges are one of the best ways to assess the quality of game in any area. The trophies on the walls are more than ornaments. They are indications of the history of the hunting grounds. The lodges always tell a silent story about the hunt.

We had come to stay at a lodge near Lake Balaton, Eastern Europe's largest freshwater lake, which would be our base for a driven wild boar hunt. Great trophies lined the walls of the dining room and hung around the fireplace. There were strong stags and tusks of wild boars, including an oddly shaped set of boar tusks. The right one was a thick twenty-four-centimeter tusk. The left one seemed endless; it was thirty-one-and-a-half centimeters. It was, and still is, the longest tusk I ever remember seeing. I had seen the Hungarian record and a few twenty-eight-centimeter sets, including one I had taken in Romania, but the magnitude of what hung on the wall of this hunting lodge in Somogy in Eastern Hungary was unmatched.

G. Huber, a German hunter, took the tusks in 2000. A reasonable person would not be wrong to conclude that Herr Huber had taken the forest's prized boar. But there is something deep and magical about the game in Hungary, as a member of the local hunting society demonstrated. He showed me photos from 2006 of some tusks with the major tooth measuring thirty-five centimeters, which are simply out-of-this-world measurements. In short, it was a good omen for me and thirteen brave souls who were to form the line for our driven boar hunt and hind shoot. Any boar of more than twenty centimeters is a solid trophy, and any boar at twenty-three or twenty-four centimeters is a gold medal.

"Boys, the boar from 2000 was a once-in-a-lifetime trophy," I said to my hunters. "The one from 2006 was even bigger! The gene pool of these two monsters is out there, and perhaps Diana the Huntress will smile on one of you."

The shoot included eight return hunters from last year's super hunt in Romania, including Steven Weiss, Bill Schaefer, Lodovico Antinori, Joe Forestieri, Brady Wyatt, Chris Wyatt, and Charles Bich. We also added Dr. Marinos Petratos, with whom I have hunted a dozen times before; Alex Knoppfler, who was just back from a successful black bear hunt in Canada; Greg Martin; Denny Levett; and Tony Lombardo from sunny California.

We were on the cusp of a good adventure. We had flown from New York via Delta. We retrieved our luggage, checked the guns through

Talking over the events of the morning's drives. (Photo as seen in the Beretta catalog.)

the always-friendly Hungarian customs, and met Toni, my partner, and Tamás, our favorite bus driver. Toni was still on crutches because he was recuperating from an injury received on a stag hunt in Romania, where he encountered one wet branch on a steep hill. It is indeed hard to watch both your step and a super stag at the same time. This is something Toni learned up close and personal. There is nothing that will send you flying straight down faster than some wet mud on a loose piece of wood or rock. We made the two-hour trip to the lodge in our Mercedes bus that held twenty-four people nicely. So with our gang of thirteen and our luggage, guns, and boots in the underbelly, we arrived at our hotel just off Lake Balaton. After unloading eight of the guns, we continued on a short distance to the hunting lodge where the other five members of the team would be staying and we would all be eating lunch and dinner together during the hunt.

The first morning at 6:30, we enjoyed our breakfast while discussing the game plan for the day. The questions are always the same from the beginners.

Question: "When do I shoot and at what?"

Answer: "Any boar without young, hinds, female mouflon, and fox."

Question: "What if I see a stag?"

Answer: "No male anything, except wild boar and roka (fox)."

Question: "Where is it safe to shoot?"

Answer: "The guides will show each gun where the best chances for animals to appear are and where it is safe to shoot."

Question: "How far will the shots be?"

Answer: "Anywhere from ten to one hundred and fifty yards; be prepared for anything."

The Rhythm of the Hunt

When standing on the line of a driven hunt, an ancient tempo comes from the forest and stretches into the field. After a few driven hunts, you learn to listen closely to the sounds of the dogs and their handlers. The dogs make a distinct sound when they see game or are on a boar. The sound is like a primordial chortle, and it is filled with delight and excitement. The handlers value dogs that are "sight loud" on game. The beaters are not immune, either. Their voices and the tempo of the beating of the bush also change when they see an animal, especially when they see a monster wild boar going to the line. The forest, too, contributes it own stanzas. The fox and hare are typically the first to flee through the line, then the hinds, and on occasion a mighty stag. The boar brings up the rear. The rifle shots are like cracking bells.

A black mass spotted in the many shades of green and brown.

On the morning of our driven boar hunt, a shot rang out against the morning silence. The beaters passed by me. No boar came, but I continued to listen and watch closely, for this is when the big boys like to run back against the line. There was nothing except the telltale smell of a nearby fox who never, quite wisely, managed to show his face. I only heard one more shot when the truck came to pick up Greg Martin and me from the last two stands. Greg had seen a hind but let it go, as he deemed it an unsafe shot. The total animal count was one hind and two missed boar. Well, it could only get better.

We all met up for a few minutes before moving on to the second drive. The line had seen boar, stag, hind, roe deer, hare, pheasant, and fox and only admitted to a couple of missed shots. As on all driven hunts, a lot of shots go off by magic. Some of the shots, which are from the keeper's guns, are identified as shots from the line by the untrained ear.

The Second Act

Moving to our next position, I was placed in a high stand overlooking a large open field just outside a big thicket. I could see eight hundred yards on each side and two hundred yards in front. With this viewpoint, I could also identify at least five animal paths exiting the brush. Yes, this would be a good stand, indeed. The beaters marched forward, and only the sight of one hare was to be my reward at this great stand.

Tony Lombardo took two boar. Steven Weiss and Dr. Mario bagged one each, and the line missed a couple more. Well, at least the ice was broken. It is the same on every type of hunt. Until you experience that first successful pheasant drive or see your stag on the ground, you are always a bit jumpy.

The second day of our hunt consisted mostly of one long five-hour drive. We settled in at the top of a high hill overlooking a four-hundred-acre thicket. There were large fields on all four sides with several roads cut out that had small openings where high stands were situated. These were perfect for observing the movements of boar, stag, roebuck, mouflon, fox, and several birds of prey. I remained up in a stand watching the same opening for most of the five hours. You train yourself for the shot by thinking of what you will do when the animal comes out. As you are waiting, you start to memorize every tree or bush that looks like a boar or a hind. At least from a stand, you may have a solid rest, which is a great advantage, as shooting from the ground is often more difficult.

After observing two distinct game trails, I descended my stand and stationed myself next to the one that seemed to have the most traffic in hopes that it would be used as an escape route. The beaters did a reverse drive, passing us and disappearing deep into the thicket. Soon, I heard the familiar sound of an animal crashing to safety slightly off to my left. Moving to see if it was a stag or hind, I already knew it wasn't a boar. After listening to the sounds a thousand and one times, you pretty much know what it is that you are hearing. Just then, a hind came directly toward me from ten feet away. As I raised my gun, she leapt right over my head! Immediately I ducked, getting a nice view of her hooves and nothing else. The drama was over so quickly that I never got a shot off. That was to be the hind's day.

After so many safaris to Africa for dangerous game and hunting everything from brown bear to jaguar, a female red deer almost wiped me out. Life is funny that way; you never know which way the dice will fall.

After telling the boys of my narrow escape at lunch with Tony Lombardo as my witness, Toni Török told a great hunting story that really belonged in a book. It seems one of our German clients had just shot a good boar when, out of nowhere, a big stag bolted directly toward him. Before the nimrod had time to react, the huge deer took his rifle right out of his hands, as the sling had hooked onto its antlers! They followed the stag's tracks for perhaps two hundred yards and found the gun lying on the ground with a broken scope and detached barrel. I guess you never know what can happen with wild animals until it actually happens! During the next couple of days, we all took a break from hunting boar, with some of the group choosing to hunt big game and some opting for sightseeing. Joey Forestieri and Alex Knoppfler both managed gold-medal fallow deer. We kept seeing fallow deer through the driven lines, so we knew the chances would be outstanding. Alex's deer had antlers that weighed more than 4.2 kilos and Joe's weighed in at a monstrous 4.56 kilos. Hungary has the best wild fallow deer hunting in the world, and these two guys helped prove the point.

Day three of our driven boar hunt produced thirty-six boar and seven hinds, making it an outstanding afternoon. My old friend Lodovico Antinori joined us for those last two days. Lodovico is a student of the roebuck, as am I. It was our passion for the little buck of the Puszta that caused our first meeting. We worked the thickets as it began to turn colder—something we had not experienced the first two days. With the cold comes the movement of animals. After a solid morning, we ate a hearty lunch out in the field on a long table. We dined on goulash, chicken, potatoes, and meat pies. A delicious sponge cake and strong hot coffee finished the meal. We didn't sit long, but allowed just enough time for the beaters and dogs to rest. The dogs are always a marvel to watch. Jack Russells, Jag hounds, and long-haired dachshunds are all true warriors against the boar, as I have witnessed firsthand numerous times.

As the afternoon rolled on, I found myself on the end of the line when a big boar surprised me. It was perhaps a bit far as I let a round

Baron Carlo Amato, Deborah Langley Horn, and David the Earl of Warrick after a day in the field.

of .30-06 220-grain Federal discharge from my Beretta 689 Silver Sable Double Rifle. I aimed for the neck and saw the brute stumble a bit just before hitting the thicket. At the end of a drive, the beaters stop by and ask what you shot and where. I explained that I hit the boar, but it might have been wounded. We headed toward the spot of the shot, and there in the thicket, I found blood. The brush was so thick that you could not see more than ten feet in front of you. The head hunter, Lazlo, sent a pack of a half-dozen yelping dogs in to search. We soon heard the sound of canines nipping on a boar about one hundred and fifty yards away. The animal broke from the thicket with the dogs hot on his heels. I let go again, bringing the boar down. However, he was not to die without a fight. He was flinging dogs everywhere. I moved in with one of the Hungarians for the coup de grace. He produced a Hungarian 9mm and handed it to me. I quickly dispatched the big boy just behind the ear, as I had done many times before when I worked at Shangri-La Wild Boar Preserve in Canada.

Each time, like the first time, your blood is boiling and adrenaline is pumping as you move in close to the boar and dogs. First, you have to back the dogs off a bit, then angle your shot down through the brain—something I learned in Africa many years before (where my handgun hunting became a passion). Up close and personal, a wounded wild boar is a thing of meanness, looking to take out a few dogs and you, if possible. Never think it is over until it is over.

As night fell, we retreated to the lodge for some dinner and a sampling of wine that Lodovico had brought from his vineyard in Italy. Let's just say, no one was moving with great speed on that next sunrise.

Up bright and early the final morning, we traveled to a different area that reminded me of England's long valleys, which consist of beautiful large fields with long thickets running down the middle. On opposite sides of the valley were rolling hills and forests that consumed the area, along with a few cornfields that boar just love. Several people commented that this area would be perfect for driven pheasant. I remarked that indeed it would, but the people who have 50 big stag, 350 boar, 35 fallow, and 125 roebuck to hunt, not to mention a couple hundred females, are not interested in small-game hunting. The efforts to raise birds and keep them around are much tougher than the needs of big game. This is one of the tragedies of Hungarian hunting. The areas that could produce truly great pheasant drives are almost exclusively used for the more profitable big game. They are using a renewable resource that takes little management when compared to pheasant or Hungarian partridge.

The last day proved to be the perfect driven boar hunt. It was the kind of day that one hears about but must be lucky to experience. I could feel and smell the boar as we passed numerous thickets, animal trails, and mud wallows. Drive after drive produced many big boar and hinds. On the second drive, I was near Lodovico, who was off to my right. Boar after boar flew past us. When the smoke cleared, we had six boar between us and a total of seventeen more for the line.

All you really need is one stand like this to say you have been on a real driven wild boar hunt. It was wonderful to see everyone smiling and each hunter with a boar. To me, this is one of the greatest forms of hunting left in the world and something every dedicated hunter who has the means should experience at least once in his or her life.

I love every kind of hunting, from rabbits on up, but there is something about waiting at a boar stand on a brisk winter morning that is truly unique. Perhaps it is the memory of taking that big boar that appeared from the fog or the lure of the unknown.

Chapter Nine

Roebuck on a Stag Hunt

When you hunt stag or any animal in Hungary, you go out each morning with only the main quarry in mind. So, it was in the famous Lábod area on a late September morning, just at the end of the stag's rut, that we were hiking out to a promising deer stand in the middle of a cornfield. My guide abruptly halted and froze. Reading his body language, I felt positive there would be at least a fourteen-point stag standing somewhere in front of me.

Sadly, there was only a little deer making his way out into the corn. I was curious to know what it was, for having little experience in my early days, it could have been a female red deer, female fallow deer, or a roebuck for all I knew. Toni gleamed, stating in a firm voice, "It is a very nice roebuck. Do you want to stalk it or continue onward to the stag stand?" I was hunting stag, even though I had already taken one from Hungary on my first trip, and I had not had a go at a roebuck. After careful consideration, knowing that this was only the second day of a ten-day hunt and having already spotted two mature stags, we decided to continue the stalk. Toni

Sunflower antlers. Photo by Mark Hennessy

felt certain that this little deer was a medal-class buck, which—unlike in Eastern Hungary—are not so numerous in this region.

After gathering our excited band, we slowly and delicately half-stepped our way toward a thick tree line on the other side of the corn-field. We hoped the roebuck would finish his morning meal and saunter out into the open, giving us an ideal vantage point. This action would allow us time to get into position for a sporting shot. As we got to the end of the field, I noticed three females standing outside the tree line. I remember wondering whether these deer were our boy's harem or not and how could we sneak past them to the safety of the trees. We crept quietly away from the group, keeping as much of the cornfield between us as a shield as possible. After about forty minutes, we finally entered the woods. Now, we were praying the big old buck had caught up with the females and would be in plain sight.

There they were, but only the three does stood silently. I located the perfect tree that had a solid rest and was approximately two hundred yards from the group. I settled in, binoculars focused clearly, and watched one side of the field while Toni watched the other. After a short time, my eyes caught a glimpse of the tips of a buck's antlers as he moved for just a second in the corn. They were thick and dark. That was all I could make out in the blink of an eye. Toni felt confident that this was the same buck we had seen go into this area, because he remembered dark antlers. He felt the buck would most likely exit the corn about one hundred and fifty yards away, a short distance from the females. I removed my binoculars, lowered myself into a solid sitting position, made sure my gun was loaded, checked my safety once again, and turned my scope to seven power. Suddenly, the deer appeared almost at the spot where Toni predicted. The buck was a perfectly formed six- or seven-year-old with antlers of more than four hundred grams. He was a monster for this part of Hungary and a fine trophy. That was good enough for me.

I slowly and quietly pushed the safety off, took a deep breath, exhaled halfway, and squeezed the trigger. The next thing I saw was three females standing in the open and no buck. Toni had heard the bullet strike true. I had the feeling of elation that one always has after a shot that worked out as planned. We cautiously walked over to the

Toni Török with a monster of Eastern Hungary—just look at those bases.

spot where the buck had been standing. We looked and looked but found no buck. Finally, after studying the area, I found some blood. We traced the blood droplets and after an hour of hard searching, found him not fifty yards from where he was hit. There was a bullet in his heart and the field of corn had completely swallowed him up. My first Hungarian roebuck hunt had been a good one indeed. It was a silver-medal effort.

After having hunted more than one hundred and twenty of these fine little bucks, I still remember that first Hungarian one as if it were yesterday. I can smell the cornfield and feel the roughness of the bark in the forest and the solid gun rest the tree provided for the perfect shot. I can also remember the tracks in the mud and the position of the buck as I pulled the trigger more than twenty years ago. I seem to never forget details of my hunts, as I do not need much prompting to retell them again and again. Oh, and by the way, the stag we were after was a sixteen-point beauty taken two days later from the stand we were on our way to when we connected with that little buck. Yes, sometimes the luck of the hunt goes completely your way.

Peter and Debbie at the end of a perfect day.

I had no idea that it was on this stag hunt that my introduction to Hungarian roebuck hunting would become an obsession, like that of the Germans, Austrians, Spanish, and French hunters. When you first see this little deer, you wonder what all the fuss is about. He is only forty pounds with antlers about ten inches high. But, like the whitetail, he soon begins to grow on you. The more you learn, the more you want to hunt him. After thirty-five years of chasing this crafty little buck, my admiration for the roe deer has yet to diminish one iota. Soon after you take a big one, you start to think about tomorrow or next year when you can once again stalk this beautiful creature. It reminds me of our love affair with the whitetail of America. You wait from year to year for just a chance at another smoker!

Well, I guess the roebuck fever is still with me, as my friends the Fenton and Hatch families will be joining me for opening day of 2013. That will make it twenty-eight years of roebuck hunting in Hungary—and still counting.

Chapter Ten

Hunting the Mighty Mountain Bear

Each time I went back to Romania, Toni and his friends would always talk about the number of big bear that live over much of the Carpathians. We went to visit his old friend Cornel near the town of Criva for a driven boar hunt hoping to be lucky enough to catch a glimpse of a mighty bruin or two. This was back in the early nineties, when we hunted as the Romanians hunted.

We stayed in a primitive sheepherder's house and ate and drank only what each of us could carry. Once off the main roads, it felt like you were in Europe the way it was before World War II. The roads were dirt and the major mode of transportation was horse-drawn carriage. When we stayed at Cornel's house, the men ate in one room while the women dined in the kitchen. This seems to be one of a number of customs left over from hundreds of years of former Ottoman rule. Our driven line consisted of police cadets, officers, and local hunters. After a successful first drive—I took three boar and a fox—I had the time of my life learning about the way of real Romanian hunting.

It was on the second drive that I saw what all the fuss was about concerning the mighty European brown bear, *Ursus arctos*. As the line of beaters was slowly approaching, I spotted something that looked like a monster boar to my left running through some thick trees. It was a huge bear that let out a growl so angry that I felt a deep primal fear in the pit of my stomach. Just behind him was another "little" bear of approximately four hundred pounds. I remember thinking, "Oh my

In this illustration, Zoltan Boros captures the essence of the mighty mountain bear.

God! I would hate to be in the way if these two boys decided to turn back on the line!"

As the drive finished and I made my way down the hill with thoughts of what I had seen, the boys were all laughing and wanted to know if the bears had come close to me. Still weak in the knees, I shot back, "Close enough, thank you!"

Never mind my close encounter, it seemed one of the truck drivers had gotten to see these bruins just a little bit better. After the bears came barreling down the hill, they changed direction and decided to follow a dry streambed that led directly to where his pickup truck was parked. The driver, upon seeing the fast approaching bears, scurried to the top of the vehicle just in time to see the dynamic duo pass within ten yards. Everyone laughed as this story was told, but it was a nervous laugh, as we all know a bear standing upright can reach the top of a truck's cab quite easily if it has a mind to. I was now determined to conquer this king of the mountains, so Toni and I planned a bear hunt for the following spring.

Gentry Beach and Chuck Ray of Dallas accompanied me on this new adventure. We flew into Bucharest and were met by Dani Gligor, our hunting representative in Romania. I had arranged to spend the first day touring the capitol, as it was my first trip to that historic area. Normally, we drove farther into Romania or flew to Timisoara, missing Romania's largest city. As a historian of sorts who always tries to learn about an area before arriving there, I did as much research as I possibly could. This way, you are able to see and enjoy the things that are really of interest to you in the short time allotted.

After satisfying our sightseeing and antiquing appetites, we were more than ready to head for the mountains to begin our hunt. We drove through ancient towns on our way up into the Carpathians. One particular spot caught our eye and lured us off our track—Dracula's Castle. "Vlad the Impaler," as Vlad Tepes was called, is actually considered a national hero in Romania. It was he who drove off the Turks in the 1450s. Author Bram Stoker was the one who turned Dracula into the monster of books and films. As Stoker was doing research for his book about the undead, he found out about this Romanian prince, who had a dark side. He had impaled thousands of Turks on the road to his castle, causing an invading Turkish army to want no part of this devil.

Another legend says that one night Vlad invited a group of nobles who had opposed him to a big dinner. This was just after he came to power and wanted to show there were no hard feelings. Once his noble guests arrived, he closed the doors and proceeded to have all of his opposition eliminated. They say he drank their blood afterward.

In the 1930s, the archaeologists dug up his grave and only found dog bones. The isolated mountains are full of superstitions of the undead. If a soul is not at rest, they drive a stake through the heart and into the coffin to keep the body from walking the earth.

Feeling a little apprehensive, we cautiously left the castle and regained our focus on the main task at hand—locating that mighty bear. After a long climb, we reached our lodge at the foot of the highest peaks. All three hunters had been previously assigned areas that were as much as one hundred miles apart. The mountains are full of bear. Romania has the best population of bruins found in Eastern Europe. There are also bear in Scandinavia and Russia, and nowadays they are even in Switzerland, Austria, and Italy. But Romania has more than the rest of Europe combined.

Preparing for the hunt, we sighted in our guns and made sure we had everything on the list I always provide for hunters as to the specifics of each hunt. Items such as a flashlight, knapsack, walking stick, water, energy bars, hand warmers, etc., all come in handy at one time or another.

The following morning, we left the lodge at 9:30. Because most of the time bear come to feed at dark, we did not have to get up very early to get to our blinds. We drove for an hour over bumpy paved roads as we slowly made our way up the mountain. Next, we transferred to a four-wheel drive Lada, as the climb had become quite steep, and proceeded another hour and a half on dirt roads. Our last hour was on foot.

Just before reaching the blind, we happened upon a mountain stream that was filled with recently melted snow and large boulders. The bridge we had to cross consisted of three fat mossy tree trunks resting sixty feet above the rushing water. I had in my arms my gun, knapsack, and a walking stick, all of which do not help when trying to cross a set of slippery logs. I had to make a decision. Had I come all this way to be turned away by sixty feet of unsure footing? Hell no! I handed my rifle over to the two guides and slowly inched my way across the unsteady span, never once looking down. It may not sound like a big deal now, but believe me, it had me thinking really hard for a second or two.

We forged on for an hour more, when through the trees I could barely make out what looked like a rooftop. I remember hoping it would be a place to rest for a while. But no, it was in fact our blind. There stood a two-room house with a big front porch built on some sturdy, thick logs that towered twenty-five feet above a meadow. Inside, there were two beds, a heater, a small kitchen, and four windows that overlooked the entire field.

Feeling tired, I sat down to rest and gathered some information from my guide, Florin, who spoke some English. He told me that he and his assistant took turns watching five different blinds to see where the big bear were coming from to devour their free treats. The bait, which was made of ripe sheep and cow, is like candy to a bear. Groups of guides in each area start looking for the good bear around March. Hunters come for the spring bear in April. So, here I was in the Carpathian Mountains in April during the full moon, looking intently out my little window for the European brown bear.

We checked weapons, windows, and supplies before settling in for the evening's watch. As the sun was barely visible behind the tree line and darkness was approaching, something moved out to the middle of the field. It was a big black monster of a thing. With my window already opened, finger on the safety, I listened for the agreed word, "OK." To my surprise, the bear turned into a large wild boar! You don't see many boar up in the high mountains, but if you do—and they have managed to elude the bear and wolf—they can be real monsters. He was at least 375 to 400 pounds of serious meat with big tusks shining in the moonlight. He proved that any boar that manages to elude the bear and the wolf is something fierce and powerful in its own right.

This lucky boar ate his dinner, then became somewhat agitated and suddenly disappeared into the woods. I watched the area where the boar had been looking, and after about five minutes, a small bear lumbered into the meadow. Florin immediately whispered that no, he was too young. We observed him for about a half hour shuffling back and forth from bait to bait. I had my gun sighted in on him several times to practice for his big brother, who I hoped would soon appear. There was still plenty of snow on the ground, so this, coupled with the full moon, let me see the bear perfectly through my scope. We took turns waiting for the big boy all that night but to no avail.

The next morning after finishing our breakfast, we set out to check for tracks and stalk several animal highways we discovered leading to and from our blind. A few sets of boar and wolf tracks caught our attention. We then spotted the hoof marks of a lone stag and the deep ruts of a really huge bear. This got everyone excited. We began talking all at once in Romanian, German, and English about the possibilities these pawprints might yield.

After a long day of stalking, we made our way back to the blind, had an early dinner, and began our serious watch. It was just after 9 p.m. that I felt Florin pushing my arm ever so slowly. He pointed to the right as we listened and peered out the window. I stared into the blackness for any sign or movement. Suddenly, Florin pushed hard on my arm. I recognized that push from the experience of a hundred hunts. He must have seen or at least heard the bear. Thirty seconds later, an enormous bruin appeared from the right, first stopping under the cover of some pines. By this time, I knew where every pathway was leading to the bait. As he stepped out into the open snow, I had already picked my spot and could see his leg stretched out in front. With my Beretta Mato .30-06 and a Zeiss scope with illuminated reticule, I had no problem zeroing in on his chest. I squeezed off the shot using a strong rest.

The bear yelled angrily in pain, then turned and quickly ran off in fourth gear. There was no time for a second shot. We struggled to see if he was going down. Florin slapped me on the back and Mihai hugged me as they both exclaimed it was a perfect shot. "The bear is very dead!" they yelled. I must admit, I did feel really good about the shot, as everyone lit up a cigarette or cigar while we waited a bit. These brown bear have a much-deserved reputation for attacking hunters, so we didn't want to rush to the scene of a dying bear. I witnessed this personally after inspecting the scars on Florin's stomach and the deep claw marks on Mihai's rifle. It seems Mihai used his rifle to ward off a dead bear who, upon being approached, decided to live a bit longer. Luckily for Mihai, he was not alone and the hunter dispatched the undead bear.

The author and a gold-medal bear taken by the full moon in Transylvania.

We climbed down from the blind with guns and flashlights at the ready. Having found plenty of blood exactly where I shot the bear made us feel even better. There was a constant blood trail in the snow, along with tracks that showed the bear had been hit on the left front.

We followed his trail to the top of a steep hill where we stopped to study his path. I could barely make out something in between the rocks at the bottom when my legs gave out, and I went sliding downward at full speed. On my way down the hill, I realized one of the rocks was a dead bear. I truly hoped he was finished as I slid to a halt with my rifle in hand at the ready. The two guides were laughing hysterically. They thought it was the funniest thing they had ever seen. I laughed with them, although it was the same kind of nervous laugh one has after an elephant or buff charge has just ended. Florin then pulled out the fire-water and we toasted this noble beast again and again.

After taking photos of the mighty brute, we sent Mihai down to bring back a sleigh. With wolves hiding in the wings, you do not want to leave any kind of meat laying out overnight if you can help. Not long after, Mihai returned with three other guides, a horse, and a sleigh. I could hear them approaching through the crystal clear mountain air quite some time before they actually came into view. It was the sound a hunter might have heard one hundred years ago.

We held a brief discussion on whether anyone had ever seen this bear before and subsequently agreed that no one had. The six of us worked in unison to load the bear onto the sleigh. The horse had obviously been used for this task previously, as he did not seem to mind. Most domesticated animals flee at the scent of a bear, let alone get close to one. I squeezed in next to the fallen bear on the sled with two hunters sitting up front and the other three guides walking just behind.

As we drove down the snow-laden path, the moon was at its fullest, and everything in the woods was visible. Without warning and out of nowhere, an ancient sound from fifty thousand campfires ago broke the dead silence. It was a pack of wolves howling at the moon—or was it at the bear carcass? I suddenly remembered an old Russian painting I had seen with wolves following a sleigh with a stag tied on the back. Cautiously, I glared in every direction as the sleigh's speed picked up just a bit. My gun was secure in my hands and ready to defend, as no stinking wolf was going to have a go at my bear or my mode of transportation, for that matter. The guides had stopped talking. Now, only the howling came periodically back to my ears. This was it. Here I was on a successful bear hunt, riding down the Carpathian Mountains on a horse-drawn sleigh, with a pack of wolves just out of sight. You cannot make up this kind of adventure. It may only come once in a lifetime, and when it does, it is yours forever.

I could now see a faint light. It was our guide's small house where we had our vehicle parked out back. We went in for some hot coffee and a bowl of hearty soup, leaving a guard outside to watch over our hard-earned trophy. At 5 a.m., we arrived back at the lodge and found out Gentry had also taken a super bear, and Chris was still out in his blind where he would spend the night. I fell asleep thinking of my bear and the howling of the wolves.

By 9 a.m., both Gentry and I were downstairs in the dining room rehashing the stories of our respective hunts over a hot breakfast. The first night Gentry also let a smaller bear go, as I had informed him of what to look for in a trophy. The second night, just as the sun was about to disappear behind the trees, this huge bear came out fifty yards from the blind. At first, the old boy had his back turned toward Gentry—not the shot you want to be taking at these big fellas. After what seemed like an hour, so probably five minutes, the animal turned broadside and Gentry let him have a shot with his .300 WM. The bear fell not thirty yards from the point of impact in full view of the smiling Texan.

Young Gentry Beach and his excellent bear.

The following day, Gentry and I decided to sit in different blinds to help watch for a bear for Chuck. We were a good forty miles from Chuck's blind, intending to narrow down the playing field as much as possible. There was no action until the next evening when Chuck came back to the lodge half-smiling. He had hit a good boar, or male bear, squarely in the shoulder. We all prayed he actually did. Just after 11 p.m., the bruin had let out a monster roar as he darted for the tree line. There was plenty of blood found where the bear had obviously stumbled. After following his trail one hundred and fifty yards or so in the thickets, the hunters wisely decided to search for him in the morning.

Everyone was up and out at the break of dawn. We scattered about, moving slowly through the woods, which were now a little more visible as the sun began to glisten against the snow. It hadn't been long when someone yelled the good news, "The bear is dead!" Not two hundred yards from where he was first spotted, a lung shot had laid him to rest. Now we had plenty of time for photos and skinning. The party that night was one to remember, but that's another story. As we had an extra day, we headed back to Bucharest for some more well-deserved sightseeing.

There is a high number of European brown bear in Romania. They are a menace and cause a lot of harm regarding both livestock and people. Each year, the bear population gets stronger and stronger and moves closer and closer to the ever-increasing human population.

Chapter Eleven

Of Sons and Stags

When my son Lee was fifteen years old, it was time for him to see my other home. I took him to Hungary to introduce him to big game hunting in Europe. Toni, my Pannonvad partner, took care of every detail. He wanted this trip to be perfect. Toni's son, Daniel, is a year younger than Lee, so Toni is an expert in keeping a teenager happy and busy on a hunt.

Lee Phips Horn with his medal-class stag.

We chose a spot above Pecs fifteen miles from the Croatian border. The Vorosalma area overflows with beautiful mountains, forests, and rolling fields. It is renowned for outstanding stag and huge wild boar. Two clients, Bob Hoover and Michael Blum, joined us.

We staycd in a small, homey hunting lodge. Our group occupied every room, so we had the entire thirty-five thousand acres all to ourselves. The first morning, we sighted in our guns. Out of everyone, Lee's shot group proved the best. I think the guides held this session just to see if this American kid could really shoot. Surprise, surprise! He was one of the best shots on his varsity rifle team—he could hit the target.

Lee was full of questions for Toni and me that night before the first hunt. "At what distance do you think I will have to shoot?" he wondered. "Will the guide tell me when to squeeze the trigger?" He did not want to shoot the wrong animal or worse, miss. Lee craved as much information as he could compute, so he would be ready for zero hour. All the doubts of a young boy that I can remember from my past came up that night. We explained to Lee that the guides were experts in the art of stag hunting, and he was in good hands. They would judge the age and size of the animal before he could shoot and signal with a "Yo," or "yes," when it was the right time to pull the trigger.

Everyone left early the next morning with their own guide. Michael Blum soon connected with the first of his two stags. Although it wasn't the biggest stag in the world, Michael smiled proudly, as your first stag so readily allows you to do. On the third day, brother Bob Hoover, who has been on seven hunts with me, shot a beautiful silver-medal beast. Continuing his hunt, "Lucky" Hoover scored a big medal-class boar on the fourth day that came out of the woods following a lone stag. He shoots a little pre-'64 Winchester .30-06 that he's used since he was seventeen. It is not the prettiest or the best fitting gun, but Bobby shoots it better than any of his fancy guns. As someone in the gun business, I am often asked what gun is the best to use for this kind of hunting or that type of shooting. My answer is always the same: whatever gun you shoot the best. Your gun should be as comfortable as a good pair of old shoes.

Continuing with our success, Michael added a gold-medal stag. I managed a nontypical with one perfectly formed antler and the other a small turned-down stump. After four gold and seven silver-medal red deer, I was ready for something different. Well, Stumpy was certainly that. Besides, I was helping to improve the stag in the area by taking this funny boy out of the gene pool.

The red deer wasn't young Lee's first member of the Cervidae *family.*

On the morning of the fifth day, Jozsef, an experienced guide, and Lee made their way through the black forest just before the sun took over. They heard a deep roar at the end of a large cornfield and decided to approach the stand closest to where the old warrior might show himself. Walking through the dark woods and listening to the stag's songs get louder and louder made Lee's heart race. As they reached the edge of the field, the foggy mist was just beginning to clear. Ever so slowly, stepping lightly from one rung to the next, they climbed the ladder of the deer stand in hopes of not giving themselves away. Lee could now settle in and get ready to meet this fella head-on if the stag ever decided to show himself. Shooting positions were staked out and the scope was set on seven power. A thick wool scarf made a suitable rest. Jozsef roared through his stag call and the ole boy responded right back, "I am coming to see who is trespassing on my turf!" As if by magic, the stag appeared in the early morning light.

The guide had to age him and gauge the size of the antlers with a certain sense of urgency, as he was just out of the forest and could step right back in the shadows of the trees with no notice. "Yo!" A medal-class stag! Lee's safety came off and the next thing he remembered was that the stag was gone. Joseph gave Lee a warm slap on the back. He had seen the big boy fall.

On this fifth day, my son became the youngest foreign hunter to take a stag in Hungary. Lee returned in triumph to the cheers of everyone back at the lodge. Now he was to be introduced into the select group of successful Hungarian stag hunters.

As this was Lee's first stag hunt, he had been bloodied. A little blood is placed on the new hunter's forehead at the time of the victory. This traditional mark shows old hunters that a new member has been admitted into their group. The magnificent animal is then laid out on the ground with evergreen branches placed in a circle around his body. Fires are built on either side. The beautiful sound of hunting horns pays tribute to the fallen animal, along with the calming words of the head guide as he blesses the animal and says, "Auf Wiedersehen!" All hunters remove their hats during this ancient ceremony. This is a time to reflect and thank the forest for giving up one of its inhabitants.

Now everyone was ready for a big celebration party for Lee's stag. All the guides came, as well as the chief hunter. We made Lee retell the story a half-dozen times—we wanted to make sure he learned the proper way of embellishing a good hunting story! One of the best times on a hunt for me is at night—sitting around the dinner table talking of the day's successes and failures. No matter how many times I go hunting, I love to hear descriptions of the day's events from the beginners to the experts. Each story reminds you of something you have once experienced.

Lee with his first trophy raccoon.

My son had his first taste of boar meat and champagne that night and slept until noon the next day. We spent the last two days looking for a good boar. Since Lee had seen nine wild boar in a field during one of his stag hunting days, we went back to that area and positioned ourselves in a stand while waiting for a tusker to cross in front of us. As dark approached, we were startled by the sound of something moving through the underbrush. There in the faint moonlight was the familiar black hump of a male boar calmly walking about.

A guide and Lee with his running boar.

I told Lee where I thought the boar would exit the undergrowth and that he would most likely be running, as the big boys usually hightail it when they hit a clear field. Suddenly, the boar appeared about two hundred yards from the stand and broke into a slow trot as he hit the open ground. While Lee waited for him to stop, I noticed the boar was already in knee-high grass just before the forest was about to swallow him up. I whispered in a calm, firm voice, "It is now or never, Lee." His .30-06 barked in the night. I saw the boar hunch up. It was a well-placed hit. He was a good hundred and seventy-five yards away in the tall grass. I did not want to have to track a boar into the woods after dark, even with three good flashlights in tow. We did not have to worry, though, as the six-year-old boar rested in his final sleep not thirty yards from where Lee had shot.

We took five stags and three wild boar in a week of hunting. It must have been Lee's beginner's luck that ran through the entire camp.

Lee has now hunted North America, South America, Africa, and Europe. He told me he best remembers being that young boy on the stag and wild boar hunt in the forests of Hungary. I remember our hunt in Hungary as if it were yesterday. On that trip, I saw him grow up a little more. As many fathers know and feel, nothing is more gratifying than time spent hunting with your son. On these trips, a bond is formed—a bond dating back millions of years to the dawn of man's existence.

Chapter Twelve

Hunting Driven Wild Boar: Really Getting into the Early Form of Hunting

———

At the dawn of time, hunters realized animals flee upon hearing, smelling, or seeing man. Driven hunting thus became one of man's first successful forms of group hunting. A line of hunters simply pushed animals toward a line of waiting spears. I was introduced to driven boar hunting in Nova Scotia, Canada, by my friend Baron Carlo Amato, who owns a wild boar preserve on Robert's Island just outside the town of Yarmouth, Nova Scotia.

One afternoon, after a successful hunt that yielded a grand old boar, Carlo suggested I run his hunts. I have professionally hunted in Sudan and was armed with quite a bit of knowledge about boar amongst Spain's monterias and many years spent on Robert's Island, so I naturally accepted. I soon realized we had a high-quality problem. There were too many boars on Robert's Island. A driven hunt was the answer to reduce the overcrowded population. We gathered a group of locals from Yarmouth to do the beating and filled the line with experienced hunters.

The wild boar seems to fly through the woods when in a dead run.

I felt exuberant during that first drive, as did Carlo. As we quietly waited, inhaling fresh morning air, we could hear the faint sound of beaters off in the distance. Everyone's hearts pounded a little harder on the line, and soon squirrels, foxes, and deer started dashing through. Then we heard a small tank crashing out of the bushes. It was a three-hundred-plus pound six-year-old male boar, followed by a female with a half-dozen young, and an even larger male brought up the rear. One of the great excitements of a driven hunt is that you never know what animal will come barreling past the line, where the first animal will appear, or how many will be in a group. After five drives in one day, we downed forty-three boar, having made sure all age groups were included in the day's bag.

This was my first taste of a new and exciting form of hunting, and I liked it. Carlo, who has much experience in these matters, suggested boar hunting in Germany and Eastern Europe. Little did the Baron know, he was the catalyst for me spending every year thereafter joining European hunting lines in pursuit of this noble swine. I experienced wild driven boar hunting in Germany, Hungary, and finally Romania. Compared to my experiences hunting the big five, bongo, and giant stag, driven boar hunting added an entirely different dimension to my hunting memories. All hunting makes my blood run quicker, but each driven boar hunt is infused with an unknown element. Every hunt is completely unique, never to be replicated.

By the late 1980s, I started hunting driven boar in Hungary. When the government opened Romania's famed Timisoara region, my partner, Toni Török, introduced me to monster boar hunting as it existed fifty years ago—before World War II forever altered Europe's ancient hunting grounds. Toni and I shared many good hunts. This lasted until 1995, when the rest of Europe discovered Timisoara and the quality of the hunts suffered. We loved the area, so we shifted to less pressured game. We spent a decade pursuing bear, roebuck, wolf, and capercaillie, never expecting to again experience driven boar hunting in those old areas. Then in 2005, for reasons that were never really clear, the government reopened some of the areas that had been closed a decade before. The game had repopulated during the decade of stewardship and no hunting pressure.

Toni arranged for us to do the first driven hunt in January 2006. We had eleven hunters from the US, Croatia, Italy, and Sweden, and we descended on Timisoara. The plane was three hours late. The drive from the airport took four hours. We arrived at the hotel at midnight. No one complained. We had traveled about eighteen hours door to door, but no one cared—that is a solid sign of real hunters. All anyone wanted to discuss was the next day. We spent much of the first night in the lobby discussing those picayune questions that invariably concern hunters. What will the stands look like? When will it be OK to shoot? How do we identify the big males? What were safe shooting directions? The more we talked, the more excited everyone became. We were in the midst of the world's best driven wild boar. Even though Toni and I have taken more than a thousand boar between us, we were up and ready four hours later as if it were our very first driven boar hunt.

We hunted the famous Cheveres area, a favorite of Nicolae Ceauşescu and the place of my first boar hunt in 1990, when I managed two gold medals. One boar tusk measured just about twenty-eight centimeters—a once-in-a-lifetime trophy. The hunting stands were simple. They were made of four-foot upright logs placed in front of a large tree stump that served as a seat. Each stand was situated just outside the forest at the beginning of a fifty-yard lane cut in the middle of the woods.

Before the first drive, everyone drew numbers for initial stand assignments. As with driven birds, when the drive is over, each gun moves up two stands and so on until your last stand. Then you move down two and repeat the sequence. It sounds like a lot of movement, but boar drives tend to be further apart than driven bird shoots, though the number of guns need for a good hunt is about equal. For a proper driven boar hunt, you need ten to fifteen guns. With fewer hunters, too many boar escape out the sides, not to mention the ones that turn back. With about fifteen guns, you create a shooting line that stretches some seven hundred yards. The line is naturally well equipped for the task at hand.

On this particular hunt, we had many different rifles on the line, including bolt actions and doubles chambered in .30-06, .300 WSM, 8x57JRS, and the perfect wild boar caliber, 9.3x74R. Everyone with magazine guns had extras or belts that made it easy to reach their bullets. I had taught the new double-rifle boys to hold two rounds between their fingers for the fastest possible reloading and hoped they would have better luck than I did the first time I tried this maneuver in the Sudan. I put two rounds into an angry elephant that had gotten our wind and did not like the smell. I was attempting to throw two more bullets into my Jefferies double when I realized there was a slight problem. The cartridges were supposed to be between my fingers, but somehow the ammo had fallen out as the big boy came calling. Luckily, he fell twenty yards in front of me, but that's another story.

At the end of the morning's first drive, "Lucky" Bob Hoover, Bill Hooks, and Steven Weiss all connected on boar, and on the second drive, eight males were knocked down. Chris Wyatt, Alan Romney, Joe Forestieri, Lodovico Antinori, Charles Bich, and I also increased the total. It was a successful morning, then time for a hearty lunch and stories of the many successes and failures of the hunt. Our meal consisted of five kinds of roasted meat

A late lunch after a day to remember. From left to right: Marinos Petratos, Peter Horn, Ludovico Antinori, Tony Lombardo, Greg Martin, and Alex Knoppfler.

that were slow-cooked over an open fire. This delicacy was enhanced by various vegetables to create a fine Romanian shish kebab. Out came the Cuban cigars—ever-present thanks to brother Romney—strong coffee, and a homemade chocolate cake. Now the stories about all the misses started to unfold.

It is quite normal to have ten boar down on a drive when you have counted more than thirty separate shots. Of course, no one answers when you ask who missed. We have come to joke that the missed shots are the magic bullets of the forest that fire on their own. I have done much driven hunting in my time, and I have missed before. Shooting too late, hitting a tree, or pulling the trigger just as the boar enters the one bush within a hundred yards all contribute to negative results. I heard a story from a fellow sportsman once about a hunter who watched a black stump for five minutes. He heard something move on the other side of the stump. He looked away and saw eight piglets running past. He quickly turned back around and the stump was gone. Looking toward the rear of the open lane, he glimpsed the large black stump, that had turned into a huge male, crossing into thick forest. He fired three shots at the disappearing stump to no avail. I have been there, and I have done that. The beauty of a driven hunt is that hunters have plenty of opportunities to learn from their mistakes and refine successful tactics.

After our hearty meal, horse-drawn carts took us back through the dark forests to our blinds, where we waited for a new adventure to unfold. This sequence of events never changes. You settle into your blind, remove your knapsack, and place your rifle firmly against the side of the blind. You adjust your sitting position to where you are the most comfortable. You check your ammo. You familiarize yourself with new surroundings. You study your hunting area—a triangle that unfurls from the center of your stand. Then the forest is quiet, and there is not a sound. Inevitably someone drops binoculars, and they hit with a thud or a clang. Everyone nervously looks around, afraid the noise of an outsider will alert the forest to the presence of intruders. Usually, there is no reverberation, so you return to staring at your section. A shot rings out somewhere down the line, and the hunt begins. It began that day in the dark forest when someone yelled and two guns took aim at a group of five boar, dropping two, while a third crashed into the underbrush and fell to a dead stop. Now the forest was alive.

Suddenly, it was my turn to shoot. A sizable trophy trotted into the open. A fourth boar fell. All this transpired in about thirty seconds. Silence comes once again. You can faintly hear the beaters deep in the forest, but you have to make sure it is really them; the noises of the woods often play tricks on your ears. When the sounds get louder and louder and shots sound down the line, it is the telltale sign of beaters and dogs approaching. Everyone knows to only shoot behind the line. When the beaters are almost in sight, it is time to lower the guns and take a final tally.

We counted twenty-one boar at the day's end and found two others that were stone dead the next morning before the start of our hunt

The end of a super day!

around Banloc.

Banloc

It was another beautiful, crisp January morning when the air feels pure and clean, and you feel thankful to be alive in this place and time. We passed the field where I took my giant stag sixteen years earlier.

Everyone was betting I would not remember the exact place I took my trophy, which was the pinnacle of my deer-hunting career. The hunting grounds covered more than fifteen thousand acres. But certain spots are yours, and you remember them. My eyes canvassed the area as we drove into the fields toward the forests in horse-drawn carriages.

"There! There!" I yelled, "By the lone tree just before the forest!" It was indeed the place where Nadra and I had taken a stag to remember. I might forget someone's name but not a spot that I still see clearly every time I retell the story of The Giant of Banloc. The stag was a seventeen-pointer with antlers weighing 15.6 kilos. It was good to hunt near an old spot, and we had two fine drives that winter morning. Everyone connected on a boar. The second drive epitomized why Romania remains renowned for boar hunting. Boar appeared regularly for thirty minutes. We saw single boars. We saw pairs of boars. We saw groups of up to eight boar every few minutes. Including a boar that turned back on the beaters and ran away from the line, we figured that single forest had fifty boar. We took down eleven or so in that drive. The boars were of such fine mass and quality that, until you see them yourself through the scope of a rifle in the forest, you think they only exist in pictures.

After a few drives, the hunters on the line become educated. The line learns to anticipate the quarry and each hunter refines his or her insights about driven boar. The results speak for themselves. On hunts with less experienced hunters, the line may take forty or fifty boar. A line of experienced guns could take more than eighty.

Those numbers are significant, but it is not uncommon to see more than three hundred boar during a multiday driven hunt in Romania's fabled Timis region, where only one hunt occurs in November and another in January. If you see some three hundred boar on a driven hunt, you have to wonder how many remain hidden from view. This is the kind of hunting learned and mastered through patience and practice.

The final number of animals taken is not a measure of the success of the hunt, though some say it is a measure of the quality of the game. The success of the hunt is measured in memories that are shared for years to come with new friends met on the line. Those memories linger long after the count has faded. What compares to standing in the crisp winter air in Romania as a black beauty crashes through the bush and breaks the dead silence of the forest? I have not found it to this day.

Chapter Thirteen

A Driven Shoot for Wild Pheasant in Romania

In 1991, just after hunting in Romania was reopened to international sportsmen, Bill Hooks, Drake Darrin, Dr. Marinos Petratos, and I journeyed to Pischia, an area of small villages outside Timisoara. We were there to hunt big game, or so we thought. As is our discipline, we scouted the area on daily walks, and we kept seeing wild pheasants like we had rarely seen before.

We were informed that this area had once been the spot of a driven pheasant shoot, and the birds that remained were all wild. Many foxes moved in afterward and could be found everywhere. I asked Toni and Dr. Ion Vava, the head hunter, if we could do a walk-up one morning. They responded by gathering local forestry school students to help run some small drives for us.

We did not really know what to expect that cold, clear November morning, but we figured we would at least have a nice change of venue. The four of us formed a line and walked through the woods at a steady pace, along with twenty-five or so young men and their dogs that carefully worked the brush. After finishing the drive and walking to the end of the forest, we counted seventeen pheasants and one fox as a great start for the day. Next, we were positioned outside another forest, where we could see game trails exiting the woods every fifty yards or so. The beaters loaded up onto the back of an Old Romanian army

Some interested onlookers.

truck and made the ride down to the end of the forest. Sounds of pheasants squawking were heard all around, as there were four cornfields surrounding the area. Soon birds began jumping up in the air off in the distance. The noises got closer and closer as something was making a quick beeline in my direction from about twenty yards in the cornfield. Judging from the sounds, movements, and what I had learned in Hungary, it was probably a fox making an exit. I could just make out a flash of red. My 12-gauge was a little in front of the expected escape route. As the furry animal came flying out, I was already swinging my Beretta SO9. In a split second, the fox rolled over in the dirt. I was proud of myself only long enough to watch Bill Hooks drop a left and right on two hens. Now, big cock birds with long tails were clearing the trees at the end of the woods mixed with some healthy looking hens. The drive produced a couple dozen pheasant and no fewer than four more foxes.

After I looked at the bag, two things became evident. First, there were a crazy amount of foxes around, and second, we had just done a drive of all wild pheasant. Toni said, "Of course they were wild," as they had not put a pheasant out in this area in around twenty years. As I walked or rode in a horse-drawn carriage between each drive, I could see where the area was once laid out for driven pheasant. When I spoke to Toni about my findings, he told me the royal family of Romania had used the forests and fields for a shoot more than seventy years ago.

The last drive of the morning produced more than sixty birds. I remember repeating over and over, "But these are wild birds!"

Lunch was held in the field on long wooden tables. Large fires were blazing to cook the soup and warm the tea. Bacon, ham, and cheese sandwiches piled high, filling several platters. All seemed like a king's fare after the perfect morning. I remember telling the boys, "You are doing something that can never be done again—a wild driven pheasant shoot—unless perhaps we could find another area like this one before the others discovered our secret."

Drake was thrilled with a beautiful fox he took on the first drive out in the afternoon. He wanted a hat made, so we sent it to the taxidermist along with the other 14 foxes, wild boar, and stags we accumulated on this unique adventure. But on this exceedingly memorable day, we took 177 pheasants and 12 foxes.

The next morning, I got up early with the guys to walk the cornfields. Luck was with us, as it was one of those perfect days with just enough wind to make the birds resemble fighter planes. Two more foxes fell to our guns, as did a fair number of super flying pheasants. We saw stags, wild boar, and fallow deer, as well. What a magical experience!

Many years later, I hunted this same area again with Toni and one of his German shorthairs. There were not as many pheasants or foxes, but we supplemented our bag with a couple of ducks, partridges, and hare. I clearly remember where we experienced our mystical driven shoot years before, as hunters seem to have a sixth sense about old areas of the hunt—something that must be left over from our beginning as hunters.

I have had many great days shooting pheasants, but these two events would go right up near the top of any nimrod's list.

High flyers.

Years later, I found an interesting old photograph in a Budapest flea market of four noble-looking gentlemen standing with their bag of three hare, three pheasant, and a half-dozen foxes. The photo made such an impact on me that it now hangs in my gunroom as a reminder of all the foxes we found shooting pheasants in Romania. The four hunters in our group were not as noble-looking as the gentlemen in the old photograph, but the look of satisfaction was exactly the same in our picture some seventy years later.

What is a Wild Pheasant?

Since all pheasants were initially introduced centuries ago from wild stock in China, it is fact that there are few genuinely wild pheasant populations that remain anywhere in the world. The United Kingdom has areas of wild birds on the Queen's estate in Sandringham and the estuaries of North Kent, where birds have bred with no help from people for decades. My dear friends the Al Tajirs have similar birds on their Scottish estate, and they, too, have wisely not supplemented their wild ones with reared birds. The great challenge with wild birds is feeding. In Scotland, strategically placed feeding plots support the birds. In any location you care to name, all wild creatures benefit from enhanced food sources that are available. Mereworth Castle, the Al Tajirs' other shoot, has a high population of rabbits, squirrels, pigeons, doves, and foxes. They breed no birds at Mereworth, but those wild birds thrive because of helpful plantings.

Khalid Al Tajir considers any pheasant wild if it was not bred in pens. There is no other way to differentiate—otherwise you would not be able to describe any bird as truly wild. The only places I know where you can shoot driven truly wild birds in Europe are England and Scotland for red grouse and Spain on a small number of shoots for partridge.

I remember the first pheasant shoots we did in Hungary in the 1980s; there were many wild birds over the guns during each and every drive. In April or May, when we would hunt for roebuck, breeding pairs of wild pheasants

Peter and Debbie dressed for the part.

hampered our every step while we looked for bucks. Now, there is as much debate on what constitutes a wild pheasant in Hungary, as in England. To me, any bird that has outsmarted the foxes, wild dogs, birds of prey, and jackal—yes, they came in through Bulgaria—for five or six months is a wild thing.

Over the past three decades, hunting and shooting have become a big business. Game is fed in the winter, and watering holes are easily accessible. Cover is planted to keep game on one's property at all costs. The purists naturally seek the wildest game, such as the Carpathian Mountain stag of Romania over the red deer found on the flats of Hungary, or the roebucks of Hungary over the deer found on islands or small places in Sweden. The list goes on and on.

I have seen much change brought about by the amount of game and the explosion of hunters, but let me tell you, getting out there in the cool morning air with the smell of a wood fire and the pine forest is still the same. It never changes, and when it does, it is time for you to quit hunting.

I remember on my first safari to Kenya in 1973, an old P.H. told me, "You should have been here in the fifties." I say to you, no matter what decade it is, the adventure of hunting always continues to be the greatest passion of all.

A pheasant and duck presentation.

Chapter Fourteen

The Capercaillie of the Carpathians

The elusive capercaillie lives high in the Carpathian Mountains of Romania. It is one of the most prized trophies in all of Europe. In Austria, you are allowed only one license in a lifetime. The hunt for this little bird that is the largest of the grouse family is often the experience of a lifetime. For us, it was almost the end of a lifetime.

After a six-hour drive from Hungary to Romania that zigzagged through Transylvania, we slept the first night in a ski resort in Brasov, then continued our journey up into the mountains. About an hour out of town, the blacktop disappeared and we were on logging roads built on steep, rocky ledges. As our Toyota truck proceeded up the long winding roads, we came upon several rocks scattered about in the narrow lane, which created immediate concerns about our safety. But we drove onward, and after a few hours we found ourselves in a traffic jam in the middle of nowhere. A huge boulder had rolled down the mountainside and stopped in the middle of the road. As we slowly drove closer, we saw people looking over the edge

The endless beauty of Eastern Europe.

of the cliff. Down below, several oversized rocks surrounded a smashed red car. We watched an emergency crew pull four lifeless bodies from the wreckage. No one spoke for a long time after seeing that. If we had left the hotel a bit earlier, we could have been the ones smashed to the ground. Big and small rocks continued to litter the road as we made our way.

It was a tense ride to meet Dragos Stefanescu, Head Inspector of Hunting for the Brasov area. From the second we met, I knew this was a fellow nimrod, which is to say a skillful hunter with a real love of hunting. When he talked of the clients I had sent him for bear, he detailed each hunt and hunter with the exact words of a master orator. There was nothing this young man did not know of our quarry, the capercaillie. His description of the winged trophy and the places they lived was as if it were out of a storybook. "You will hunt your capercaillie near the door of the wind," he would chant. His described our bird as black as night with brown wings, fire red around the eyes, white spots on its sides, and a tail with white marks that resemble Chinese characters. His beak is hooked like a bird of prey.

When singing his mating call, there is no way to really describe it, as the song is quite unlike anything else. First, you hear a clicking sound—two clicks each time—then a pop like that of a wine bottle being uncorked, and finally a cascading sound completes the song. The male repeats this pattern four times. The capercaillie is saying, "I am the biggest guy in the woods, and this is my fine song. I am strong and the best of all the males, so others better stay away." If prompted, this bird fights with its beak, wings, and feet.

We left at midnight after going to sleep at 6 p.m. Brother Alan Romney and I drove to one area, while Bill Schaefer and Chris Wyatt headed to another. After a two-and-a-half hour ride on mountain logging roads, our vehicle suddenly stopped. "Sounds like a fuel line problem," Alan surmised. Having worked on the truck for an hour to no avail, I disappointingly stated, "Sounds like we are not going hunting today. If you are not in place by 5:15 a.m., your hunt is over." And so it was.

Dragos, upon returning with Chris, Uncle Billy, and two huge capercaillie, could not believe our luck. As the saying goes in Romania, "The luck of the hunter depends on the goodness of his heart." (Gee, and I thought I was basically a nice guy.) Bill and Chris had the most vivid stories to tell about their adventures hunting this mountain bird.

They continually talked about all the climbing that was done in waist-deep snow, which is supposed to be gone by April. Both of these hunters are in excellent shape, so Alan and I stared at each other with that what-have-we-gotten-ourselves-into look. They were completely soaked from several falls in the snow, but they had their birds and declared that every step was well worth it. Once the hunt is over and the capercaillie is in your hands, the cold, snow, and aching muscles all seem to disappear. Bill's bird was at ninety yards in the proverbial pine tree, and Chris found his while crawling through the snow at just twenty yards. After hearing about my two friends' success stories, I was more than ready to give it a second try.

That same day, we all left in two cars and headed toward a woodcutter's house near the capercaillie area. We were hoping to help lady luck along by sleeping up in the mountains to be closer to our quarry in the early morning. This maneuver would save us several hours of traveling on tough mountain roads. Well, it seemed our week continued on a downhill spiral, as we ended up driving two and a half hours back up the steep dirt roads. Hoping to divert any problems, Dragos had a tractor at our disposal to pull the two vehicles through any rough spots, such as the worst hill where there was still deep snow. As there was still too much snow and ice, we proceeded on foot, leaving behind the tractor that was now totally stuck.

Heading toward the woodcutter's house, located by the beautiful lake of the eagle, our group climbed the mountain for more than two hours when we spotted a roof we sincerely hoped would be the lodge. Instead, to our surprise, the guide informed us it was a sheepherder's cabin. He suggested we wait there, and he would go back and see what had happened to our transportation. Well, Alan and I pulled out our water and chocolate bars and made ourselves comfortable. I went out to get some wood from a shed behind the house and noticed some animal tracks. As I was cold and my mind was on making a warm fire, I did not study them for any length of time. However, upon returning with an armful of wood, I had a moment to look at some fresh spoor. Hello! They were brown bear tracks! Upon reaching the cabin, I told Alan of my discovery, and we both laughed at the same time, agreeing to keep our rifles closer. Although I do not know how a couple of .22-250s would have stood the test of a charging eight-hundred-pound bear! There was no further excitement until the others returned a couple of hours later. We left the cars by the sheepherder's place and began the second part of the trip.

We marched toward the final woodcutter's cabin in the moonlight. The wind—at the "door of the wind"—lived up to its name as a constant, gale-like force hit us for a good hour or so. Upon reaching the house, we were both pleasantly surprised. Two of the guides had gone ahead to prepare the fire and a beautiful hunter's dinner was lavishly displayed on the table. After a hearty supper, some local brew, and a good Cuban cigar for Alan, we were off for a well-earned good night's sleep in our comfortable beds. By 3:15 a.m., we were up and moving and out the door at 4. The walk to the forest took about an hour in the dark. The reflection from the full moon made the going easier—we could actually see where we were climbing on the side of the mountain.

A capercaillie sings. Illustration by Zoltan Boros

I had studied everything I could find about this elusive bird before we came to Romania. Once in the country, we discovered many other fine points about our quarry from people who lived among the birds. The capercaillie weighs between six and eight kilos. A bird with eighteen or nineteen tail feathers is average, twenty is very good, and twenty-one or twenty-two feathers is great. The season to hunt them is April 1 to May 5, with April 20 to 26 being perfect. Now was our time, so we had our guides check the areas along the pine trees for any concentrated droppings, as well as locations containing both old and new tracks.

As we cleared the last of the open, snowy meadows, we began to descend into the pine forest, home of the capercaillie. Each hunter was carrying a Tikka .22-250 with a Burris 3x9 scope. The guide had a 12-gauge shotgun, just in case a shot was made within twenty yards and not one hundred fifty yards, when a male can be caught on the ground in an open field. We moved past trees with bird droppings scattered below them and spotted some tracks. Assuredly, I thought, this must be the place. Suddenly, Dragos stopped dead in his tracks. He was listening to something way off in the distance. It was the call he had been telling me about.

When the bird sings, you move, as this is when he cannot see or hear you. When he stops, you stop. If he continues to call, you move again. We slowly moved up the side of a pine-covered mountain using this technique. Now, we could hear two birds. As with the roar of stags, the hunter quickly determines the older bird. Stalking this capercaillie was the longest forty minutes of my life! At 6:40 a.m., Dragos pointed out a tree just ahead. I saw nothing but an extremely thick pine tree. Searching and squinting, the only thing I could focus on was pine needles. Then, peering through my Burris scope, I picked up on the movement of a head and soon after, a body. My illuminated crosshair found the chest of this mighty bird, and in the flash of a second it was all over.

Alan Romney and Peter Horn, completely exhausted but completely happy.

What a sense of accomplishment for a hunter! It was the same high I got from each of my bongo hunts—to give you some idea of how I rank this magnificent trophy. We took some photographs, rested a bit, and walked out in what seemed like half the time it took to walk in. Such is the magic of all successful hunts. The full impact of this adventure didn't sink in until we reached the hunting lodge more than four hours later. I had just spent the last seven months going through treatment and recuperating from throat cancer. During that whole time, I lived for this day. The doctors assured me everything was fine, and I had walked several days in the icy snow at seven thousand feet just to prove it.

After well more than sixty trips to Africa and one hundred sixty other hunts, this capercaillie was one of my greatest sporting achievements.

We all sat around the fireplace telling our stories of the hunt. Each hunter now knew in his heart the meaning of this truly special bird. It is funny to think that after hunting such unique and dangerous game as Cape buffalo, elephant, brown bear, bongo, ibex, and yellow-back duiker that this king of the European game birds is treasured among my greatest accomplishments. Until you hunt an actual species, you have no way of knowing what memories will remain in your heart. No book or video will help you foresee your personal moment of truth with an unfamiliar quarry in a land that is often just as unfamiliar.

Next, we headed off to Bucharest for some sightseeing and on to Budapest, where I did some quick shopping at Kettner—my favorite hunting store—and the antique market just outside the city. The following day was spent visiting a new area that Toni and I were contemplating using for our fall driven pheasant shoots and a new duck area we were considering for a hunt the following October. We finished our last meeting at the airport by putting together a group for Hungarian partridge in 2007 at the estate of my good friend, Marques Lodovico Antinori. I love planning the next hunt, as it always promises a new adventure. It is what keeps me coming back again and again.

Footnote: 2011 was the last year of hunting this magnificent bird in Romania. According to the Romanian Game Department, with all the logging going on, the capercaillie's habitat had been disappearing at an alarming rate. As all good things come to an end, I count myself lucky enough to be among the few Americans with the opportunity to experience this now-vanished piece of hunting in the Carpathian Mountains.

All smiles.

Chapter Fifteen

An All-Ladies Roebuck Hunt

Sandy Froman, the first female NRA President; Nicole Capossela, Director of NRA Corporate and Foundation Relations; Debbie Horn; and I first talked at the Safari Club International Show in 2007 of hosting an all–ladies roebuck hunt in Hungary.

As the NRA ladies browsed through some of the Beretta Gallery hunt albums, they came across one particular group that contained a plethora of female hunters. This trip was from 2006 and consisted of four couples. With all eight members hunting, half of the shooters were women. The gals making up this list were Nancy Bollman of Sanctuary fame; Pamela Atwood, one of the most recognizable female hunters in the world; Lisabeth Davis of New Mexico, who was no stranger to pulling the trigger; and of course, my own Debbie Horn, who fit right in with both experience and reputation. This was exactly the kind of hunt that seemed to entice the NRA group to run one of their own.

As we talked, it became more evident that we would all meet once again on the shores of the Danube in beautiful Budapest. I showed them more photos of twenty-plus years of past hunts, and their eyes dilated wider with every picture. Even Debbie's peepers showed a memory of past days spent afield in the best roebuck hunting country in all of Europe.

The next thing I knew, we were all meeting up at the JFK Delta lounge one evening in April 2009. I had met most of the ladies

The photo tells the story.

prior to the trip, but not Megan Guegan, the NRA Director of Communications, nor Michael Ives, the photographer. It was then and there that I knew it was going to be a great expedition. Everyone, new and old friends, soon melted into the mold of the hunter's world.

After a direct Delta flight from JFK to Budapest, we cleared customs and received our gun licenses. Everyone settled in on the bus for our three-hour drive to the countryside, either relaxing and taking in the view or sneaking in a catnap or two. The area around Lake Balaton and the several beautiful well-known vineyards nearby always makes me feel like I am home—mind you, that is after ninety or so trips.

To get the blood flowing and excitement in the air, I always like to play a little game with my groups. The first one to spot a roebuck before we reach the lodge wins a bottle of wine. Just twenty minutes out of Budapest, you better start keeping a sharp eye out for these wily little bucks of Hungary, for they may be anywhere. Bonita Fraim won the bottle of Bull's Blood about thirty-five minutes out of the capital.

We soon arrived in Lábod, and at our lodge on one of the most famous hunting areas in all of Eastern Europe, with great anticipation. It is the ancestral home of Count Széchenyi, one of the most well-known Hungarian hunters of all time. His sporting books are still some of the most popular editions found in Eastern Europe. I had the group stay at his lodge because I wanted to give them the full flavor of Hungarian hunting as it was more than a century ago.

The group sat down for lunch to a magnificent spread of what was to be the first of many plates of Hungarian country fare. Soon after, everyone unpacked and prepared their gear for the 4:30 wake-up call the next morning. We then proceeded out to the rifle range to sight in all the guns. I always tell my clients to never go out hunting immediately after arriving without making sure their weapon is zeroed in. This is especially true when your target is only forty or fifty pounds. Believe me, you don't want to try one of these babies at three hundred yards without complete confidence in your gun.

Toni leads the ladies in a toast to the guides.

The lodge near Lábod is truly something to behold with world-record class stag heads decorating the halls and hand-painted murals of red deer in the field. Roebuck, wild boar, and fallow deer also adorn the walls. Over the entrance, one can't help but notice the Széchenyi family coat of arms, which brings one back to a time where the ancient tradition of hunting was in full swing. One of the comments that I heard from every member of the expedition was the mentioning of tradition and honor always being paid to the fallen game, a practice that came from Germany through Austria and finally to the Austro-Hungarian Empire—once the splendor of Hungary.

Sandy Froman came in with a nice buck the first morning, as did Sara Potterfield of Midway USA. The afternoon saw Ann Draper of the Bear Mountain Ranch collect her first trophy, as well. The enthusiasm of these Dianas set the tone as each hunter connected on their quarry. It was like hiring your own group of cheerleaders that would run out from all sides of the lodge at any hour to hear the results of each and every hunt. At dinner, we had many a stimulating conversation about the traditions of Hungarian hunting as compared with the rest of Europe. We also talked about rifle cartridges, equipment, and future trips to Romania and points east. The most memorable conversations for me were about our Second Amendment rights. Every one of the group really made me remember yet again what we could all stand to lose as Americans. I remember asking, "If they could change the Second, why not the First Amendment, as well?"

On the second day, Bonita Fraim and Sheila Ingram came back with their trophies. Some of the other women returned with their second roebuck or a boar, helping to up the trophy count nicely.

Jill Nosler Bailey—just the sweetest gal—had this to say about her experience: "The roebuck was a truly challenging animal for a hunter like me. Shot placement on these small animals requires a steady hand." She was impressed by the traditions of the hunt, as well. When she took her first buck, the guide turned his back on the animal so it could die in peace. Respect for all animals is important in Hungary. At the end of the hunt, the hunters, guides, and animals were honored with blowing of hunting horns and illustrious speeches.

One of the highlights of the trip that Jill mentioned to me was coming back to the lodge after each hunt and hearing everyone's stories. There are certain things that make lasting impressions on each trip. I remember Nicole Capossela returning with her first buck. It was as if she had won the Olympics. The bright face and enthusiasm of her retelling of the hunt was truly something to behold. It is things such as this that make me remember why I still need to put together hunting trips after thirty-some odd years.

One of my favorite hunters to watch was Brenda Potterfield of Midway USA. She was so focused on getting her trophy. Each time she returned empty-handed, I could see her become even more intense for the next outing. Then, as if by magic, Brenda had the luck of St. Hubertus smile upon her as she took not only her first buck but a boar, as well.

Of course, I took special pride when my bride, Debbie, showed up with a beautiful old buck and a super shot was quite evident. Having an experienced Hungary hand such as Debbie along really made my job easier. Whether the shots were fifty yards or three hundred fifty yards, the ladies answered the call each time.

Peter guided Debbie to this fine buck, taken with a Tikka T-3 in .270 WSM.

Toni Török and I searched different areas each day looking for possible trophies for the group. While walking around, we spotted several promising locations to sit for wild boar. The group managed three boar, which are always a most welcomed addition to any roebuck hunt.

The ladies did not take many big wild boar, which are known to inhabit almost every forest in Hungary. This was because we only stayed out on the stands until 8 or 9 p.m. due to the fact that our guides and hunters had to catch four or five hours of sleep before going out for our main quarry. When seriously hunting boar, you stay out late into the light of the full moon waiting for one of the denizens of the deep forest to cross an open field just in reach for a shot from your twenty-foot high blind. Like all hunts, if you want the big boy, you have to narrow the playing field down the best you can.

There is always the chance of boar on any roebuck hunt.

Michael Ives was my hero on the trip, as his sense of not only the hunt but also of the beauty of Hungary was captured through his photographic efforts every day. When you have a professional such as Michael Ives along, you get quite a different perspective from the normal dead zoo photos.

On the third day, we headed into Keszthely, a famous town on Lake Balaton. Here, we visited the Baroque Fesztetics Castle and the new hunting museum, which was built with SCI Hungarian and EU funds. The hand of Zoltan Boros, who did all the wonderful murals in the museum, did the sketches in this book, as well. I always find a side trip such as this is a good way to fill in the free time you have when not hunting.

Before saying goodbye to Lábod, we ended the hunt with eighteen roebucks and three wild boar. This was the last year any of my groups— or anyone else, for that matter—would be staying in this lodge, as the

Benetton family (yes, the clothing people) had bought the place and some of the surrounding land. The good news is that much of this famous hunting area is still open to hunters.

We next headed back to Budapest and the wonderful Le Meridien. This hotel has been the Beretta and Pannonvad base of operations for the past ten years with good reason; the service and staff are the best in all of Hungary. After some sightseeing and antiquing, we had a wonderful dinner hosted by longtime friends of the NRA, Doug and Kati Lynn, who just happened to be in Hungary the same week.

A happy Jill Nosler Bailey with buck taken with a Nosler Model 48.

I must say, this was one of the most perfect hunts I have ever had the pleasure to lead. Everyone was upbeat with no constant pressure to take specific trophies. The group seemed to love every aspect of the experience.

Chapter Sixteen

Couples Hunting Roebuck

The hunting world is often thought of as a fraternity of men with similar goals who come together at specific times year after year in various places around the world. This may be true, of course, but it is not reflective of the fulfilling friendships in the hunting community. After years of promising we would all hunt Hungary together, our old friends from Safari Club International Pat and Nancy Bollman, Debbie, and I made it happen in 2006. Pat and Nancy own the famous Sanctuary whitetail operation in Michigan. Pamela and Stanford Atwood of California also joined us. Pamela is probably the best-known female hunter ever produced by Safari Club International, and Stan is no slouch either. Rounding up our team of eight hunters were Lizabette and Frank Davis of New Mexico, who are also veterans of many big game hunts.

Our group was not unique in that some wives were shooting, but rather that all the wives were hunting. These gals are all experienced in everything from the big five to brown bear and argali sheep to bongo. When we arrived with four women nimrods, the guides did not know what to expect. Only Debbie had hunted in Hungary before, shooting stag, wild boar, and driven birds.

We arrived in the early evening before the opening day for roebuck at the new lodge that is owned by my longtime friend Miklós Támba. This area consistently turns out some of the largest trophy roe deer in the world. Hungary has produced numerous world-record roebucks, and it is in our hunting block near Debrecen that monsters are taken each and every year. In one of Miklós's areas in 2004, an 810-gram buck was

Pamela Atwood with a perfect buck.

brought down. Chris Wyatt, one of our hunters, took the heaviest buck in all of Hungary back in 2003 at 758 grams. In 2005, we collected more than a dozen gold medals in the opening week. Heads of 675, 654, 636, 611, and 603 grams all came from our first group alone. Just so you understand, a 500-gram roebuck is considered comparable to a Boone and Crocket whitetail. Once you reach 600 grams, it becomes a once-in-a-lifetime hunt.

Before dinner, everyone met the guides to determine plans for the next day, which would begin at 4:30 a.m. I think the guides were wary of taking four women out on the opening day—when all the old bucks had not been hunted yet—since that first shot is the most important.

The morning air held a mist from the rain the night before. I always love stalking through the fields and forests at this time. You never know what will appear out of the fog as if by magic. In this area, I had seen more than one hundred fifty deer in the two days before the season opened by just driving or walking to scout the fields.

By midday, Pamela and Stan each took a gold-medal deer. Pat and Debbie each had silver, I had a bronze medal, and unfortunately, Nancy saw nothing worth pulling the trigger on. It was now time for one of those "light" Hungarian lunches where we regaled each other with the day's exploits. No one

Stan Atwood is all smiles after taking his medal-class roebuck.

could believe how many big roebucks were about, which is the same reaction we get every year. Until you actually see it for yourself, there is no way to comprehend this hunter's paradise.

Between the six hunters staying in our lodge, twenty-five trophy roebuck were sighted on the first morning. The Davis's report was similar. Frank managed a gold medal, while Lizabette took silver after looking over a half-dozen mature bucks.

Each day, we drove from twenty to sixty minutes in different directions to the homes of these wily little bucks. All the guides know what deer are in their area. They study them every day to watch where the mature ones spend time. There are always at least two more guides on watch in each area studying the movement of the deer. They only look for bucks that are five years or older. Thick antlers and big bases with lots of pearling are carefully noted. They also look for abnormal bucks that have to be culled, along with the killer bucks that have antlers with no branches, because they act as spears during rut fights.

On the second day of our hunt, the head guide pulled Toni and me aside to say they had spotted the deer I had not been able to get the year before. He was a big one, as I remember, with a bit of the luck of the Irish in him. After I had seen him on opening day of last year at eight hundred yards with no chance for a stalk, I spent the next six days never again catching a glimpse of him. An Austrian hunter had his safety on, a German missed clean at more than three hundred meters, and an American saw him just at last light. So far the score was big buck four and hunters nothing. I decided to let Debbie have a go at him, as he was big but supposedly not bigger than a couple bucks I had taken over the last several years.

It was around 1 p.m. when I returned to the lodge after connecting on a nice medal-class buck. There were already two other trucks parked in the driveway as I drove up beside them. One vehicle was Pamela's, who had taken her second Hungarian gold-medal roebuck, and the other truck was Debbie's, which had a large medal-class buck in the back. I remembered being happy and proud as I looked closely at the thick antlers. It would indeed go close to five hundred and fifty grams and was a trophy to remember.

As I entered the lodge, I came upon Debbie and Pamela, who were having tea and chatting about their morning hunts. It seemed Pamela made a

Pat Bollman and Debbie Horn with a symmetrical set of antlers.

nice stalk along a railroad bed to get up on a huge buck that crossed over the iron rail for the last time. She also saw several more trophy deer, but none would measure up to the area's high standards. I asked Debbie if that was her roebuck in the back of the truck, and she excitedly said that it was indeed. After I made a big fuss over the beauty of the trophy, Debbie pulled me aside and whispered in my ear, "Did you see my other buck? I took two deer!" She informed me that it was laying outside on the table by the front porch, and by the way, it was the big one! I moved right out the door, through the dining room, onto the porch, and there on the table was a monster of a roebuck. It was not only long and thick but wide as well, with exceptional points. This was the kind of deer that is celebrated in stories. I was in shock, as this was the holy grail of roebuck—650 to 675 grams of magic deer—the ones you hear about, maybe even see for a millisecond once in twenty or so years of serious roe deer hunting. I remember saying exactly the same thing to Debbie as Toni said to me fifteen years earlier in Romania. I had just shot one of the largest stags ever taken in that country, and all Toni could say was, "What did you do? What did you do?" Those were the exact words I kept repeating to Debbie. I think she thought she had done something wrong but no, it was all I could manage to get out of my mouth.

It seems they spotted this big boy after a short walk along a hedgerow by a large kale field. Tamás, Debbie's guide and my longtime buddy, motioned to her that she was to attempt the shot, although she did not know this was the big one. As Debbie rested her Tikka on a tree and looked through the Burris scope, the buck seemed small and far away. Tamás said it was fewer than two hundred yards, but it looked like three hundred fifty yards to Deb. Long story short, she shot right over the top front of the monster buck's body. Tamás was now upset, to say the least, for this deer truly seemed to have a charmed life—big buck: five, hunters: zero.

As with every story, there is more than meets the eye. It seems I had traded Debbie my Tikka T-3 .300 WSM with a Burris 3-12X Black Diamond scope, which was a bit too short for her. I remember saying, "Do you know how everything on this gun works?"

She replied, "I will figure it out. How hard can it be?" Well, the scope was set at three power from the day before when I almost had a shot on a running boar. Debbie never thought to check where the magnification was set and assumed everything was set to go. The roebuck that appeared to be three hundred fifty yards was actually two hundred yards, resulting in the high shot. The big buck bolted safely into the woods. Debbie felt this must have been a pretty good-sized buck, as she could sense the disappointment in her guide and knew they would probably never get another chance to see him again. The old boys seldom give you a second look.

Debbie and Tamás headed off to a new area in hopes of finding another large buck. As they came to a beautiful open expanse far across the glistening lake, there at one hundred thirty yards stood a 550-gram buck. This time before attempting the shot, Debbie pointed to her scope and tried to relay the message to her guide that she couldn't see clearly. After adjusting the power, Deb had her gold medal but had lost the storybook deer through human error and a bit of bad luck.

Debbie was happy with the deer she shot, and she didn't know the first one she missed was actually the big one. Tamás seemed pleased as he loaded the deer into the back of the truck. They slowly headed back through the fields toward the road. As they were passing the area where the first buck had been spotted, Tamás noticed a dark shadow standing just inside the tree line. He motioned quickly that they were to begin a stalk to get a little closer.

Peter, Debbie, and Toni with some monsters of the Puszta.

Debbie said she was a bit confused because after taking one nice buck, she thought her hunt was over, because I had told her before the trip that she would be looking for a big roebuck. Also, because her guide did not speak any English, Debbie couldn't ask him why they were taking another deer. Without a moment to communicate, Tamás motioned that it was now time to take aim. With one smooth squeeze of the trigger, the big guy collapsed to the ground, never moving an inch. Tamás let out a big Hungarian scream. As the two of them approached the animal, its antlers kept getting bigger and bigger. By the reaction of Debbie's guide, she now knew they had found something truly special. To her amazement, she realized it was the same deer she had missed earlier, but she still didn't know it was the one everybody had been talking about. I had told Tamás that Debbie should try for the big one. Who would have ever thought two roebucks of this size would be frequenting the same neck of the woods?

I said to my wife, only half-joking, no more big bucks! Well, of course, that didn't stop her, but that's another story.

On the third day, we realized everyone had taken at least three good bucks except Nancy. Now, this is crazy for an area that has nothing but good bucks. I decided to join Nancy that afternoon to change her luck. Well, the gypsies must have been working overtime on a hex for her because there was not one deer worth taking. Next, it was Pat's turn. On the fourth day, he decided to accompany his wife in hopes of finding that special deer. The spell was broken as they came in with not one but two trophy deer. I'll say it again, when it comes to hunting, I would rather be lucky than good. Because at times it is luck far more than skill, which Pat has plenty of, that lands the trophy.

Everyone was commenting on all the big boys that seemed to be roaming everywhere. I mentioned that each day it would get harder and harder to find them. I remember looking at the group's bag on that last morning while the trophy committee was scoring them. I had rarely seen so many medal-class bucks taken on a single hunt. Just then, the Davises showed up and added a few more giant antlers to the measurement list.

The Bollmans, Horns, and Atwoods with some of our combined effort.

After another memorable hunt, we finished this Hungarian trip—as we always do—with an excursion to Budapest, my adopted city. It was now time to do some serious shopping, sightseeing, and even sneak into a night at the opera *Aida*. Debbie knows the great clothing and souvenir shops all too well by now. I am in charge of the hunting stores and sightseeing. We always take our hunters to the endless antiquing areas found in and around the city, as our mutual love for the old stuff is quite evident in our New York City apartment and country house.

As the Davises headed home early, the remaining six of our group toured, ate, and shopped nonstop, then rested at our favorite inn, the Le Meridien Hotel. Since Debbie and I had just spent a glorious week in Austria, mostly Salzburg, before this fantastic roebuck hunt, we all agreed to begin another trip starting there (it's such a storybook town) before heading on to our next Hungarian adventure.

Chapter Seventeen

The King's Shoot

We have hosted no fewer than six shoots and hunts for Ken Behring, who always seems to be hunting somewhere. Ken continuously brings famous hunters along to complete the line. It is not uncommon to encounter the chief executives of the world's largest companies, senior military officials, and hunters whose prowess have made them internationally famous. You never really know who might come in on Behring's jet, so I suppose I should not have been surprised when he called to say Juan Carlos, the King of Spain, would join him on a shoot.

King Juan Carlos of Spain and the Marquis Alberto Alcorcón.

I had heard many good things about the King from a number of people who have had the honor of shooting with his Majesty over the years. Now my hunting company, Pannonvad, would learn as much about hosting a sporting King. It is always important to make sure hunters have a great shoot, but a person of such importance requires an even more bespoke experience because of the requirements for security and extra staff. We arranged for the airport in Debrecen to be at our disposal. The airport was an old MIG base. Bunkers and several Russian barracks still stood. We organized Hungarian and Spanish security details and arranged for a senior customs official to first clear Ken's plane, then the King's, which came in a couple hours later.

I had an idea of his Majesty from my old friend Fernando "Nano" Saiz, who has shot with the King on a number of occasions. What I did not know was that the King would prove to be a most charming gentleman and a sportsman of the first caliber. He graciously greeted not just the dignitaries and other high-ranking people who turned out for his arrival, but also everyone who was there, including baggage handlers.

We stayed at the hotel Hodi, an old manor house Toni and I had discovered years earlier. The place is furnished with antiques, as well as an indoor pool and bar in the basement. That first night hosting the King we had a super time at dinner getting to know everyone. I remember talking with the King about many of the same places we had hunted and shot over the years. We learned that we had many friends in common who share our love of hunting. Lord, what stories Juan Carlos told. He described them with a great flair, I must say.

The first morning we shot pheasant. The King's good friend the Marquis Alberto Alcocer proudly showed me the pair of Kemen shotguns the King just had built. They were titanium with some serious wood. He asked me how the Kemen shotgun compared with the Beretta SO6 titanium guns, which was a seemingly simple question but one that required a great deal of tact, as I was betwixt the King of Spain and other Spanish noblemen, who knew all too well of the great historic rivalries between the gun makers of Spain and Italy. My answer was simple; some may say my answer was even diplomatic.

I told the King that I had no idea Kemen was making such an excellent gun out of the newest metal available, and I would compare them favorably with any other shotguns of the finest quality. The King

The ever-present hunting horn.

did me the honor of letting me shoot his Kemens on a drive, and they were super, but I must confess that I prefer my pair of Beretta Jubilees. It is not because Cavaliere Ugo Gussalli Beretta personally picked out the wood for my matched pair or that Giulio Timpini engraved special one-of-a-kind scenes of the birds of Hungary, but it is because I love the Beretta feel. I love the way the shotguns come up and swing to the target. It has absolutely nothing to do with the fact that I have worked for Beretta going on sixteen years—I just happen to like the product. I owned a pair of magnificent Browning shotguns made for King Mihai Hohenzollern of Romania that I shot for many years and loved. But upon receiving my Berettas, I sold the Browning shotguns knowing this pair was to be my pair.

His Majesty greatly admired my pair of Jubilees, saying after close inspection and with a twinkle in his eye, "You must know someone at Beretta." I had the honor of shooting next to the King that day. Should you have the honor, let me give you some advice. Do not wait to shoot.

Juan Carlos can knock birds out of the sky from extremely far away. Shooting between the Marquis and the King can be, to say the least, a humbling experience. You better not wait to see exactly whose bird it is, or you will be looking at floating feathers. Once I got the game down, I held my own nicely, thank you very much. It was a good day. We lunched outdoors on picnic tables at a site where the flags of Spain, Hungary, and the United States were proudly displayed. We finished the day with two more super drives in the afternoon.

Up early the next day, we moved out for flighted ducks. The King asked which chokes to use, and I informed him full and extra full would be just enough. We took some challenging birds that day. There is nothing like watching a high duck fold, as it seems to stop in midair.

On the way to the duck blinds.

Juan Carlos had been admiring the famous Hungarian Vizslas that retrieved the ducks, as they worked with the same ease they displayed on our pheasant shoot. We brought Toni into the conversation as his Majesty wondered if we knew where to find a good pair of these fine hunters. It took a bit of time, but we were able to secure an exquisite pair for the royal kennels. In the evening, we enjoyed an elegant dinner with all the local bigwigs in attendance. There was plenty of good wine, food, and just a little too much toasting back and forth that ran into my valuable sleeping time. The following morning, we left early for a long drive to a wild boar area. A small special driven hunt was held for the King that produced several nice trophies.

The last day we were out for pheasant again. The shooting party was all on their game by now, and many birds fell to the line. Lunch was our ending meal, and the King presented me with a box of Cuban cigars that had been made especially for him. I watched as Juan Carlos talked to every gamekeeper, waiter, and dog handler one by one. I had shot with princes, earls, marquis, counts, and barons, but the King impressed me most. He epitomized that wonderful line from Kipling's poem *If*, which so wonderfully describes what it means to be a man and a gentlemen. "If you can walk with the crowd and keep your virtue," Kipling wrote, "or walk with Kings—nor lose the common touch." This is how I will remember my hunt with King Juan Carlos, a true gentleman and sportsman.

The Tablo de la Chasse after a fine duck day.

Chapter Eighteen

Monarchs in the Land of Kings

By Brett Parker

Brett Parker with a trophy that weighed more than eleven kilograms.

I know the great pleasure of hunting in Europe. I have enjoyed this privilege more than once, but one hunt stands above the rest. The experience was so pure and perfect that it embodies the essence of European hunting.

Peter Horn, a longtime family friend, invited my father and me on a red stag hunt in Hungary. When Peter calls about a hunting opportunity, you listen. The hunt was to be an early September affair in Csöprönd, Lábod. This area is a subsection of the famed Lábod forestry. Lábod is well known as Europe's best stag area, as it produces many gold-medal stags year after year. Our hunt would coincide with the peak of the roar, which is to stag hunting what the rut is to whitetail hunting or bugling is to elk hunting. Typically, getting into such prime hunting grounds requires many years on a waiting list. Fortunately for me, I know Peter. Since he and his wife, Debbie, would be unable to make the trip, there was room for my favorite hunting partner, my father, and me.

Csöprönd is composed of more than fifteen thousand mostly flat acres. The land is split between hardwood forest and agricultural uses ranging from corn to sunflowers. European timberlands are unlike what we know in the United States. With limited areas for production and lumber being the main export crop for the country, forestry management is intense. For this reason, the forests are almost entirely void of undergrowth. The trees are in rows so neat that it is hard to believe, and those trees that fail to grow tall and straight are removed through a culling process not unlike the one used for game management. This leaves the forests eminently huntable, and it gives the hunter a marvelous opportunity to spot and stalk his quarry.

My adventure began as many do—with the planning of the kit. I find this to be one of the more enjoyable parts of any major hunting trip. It allows the hunter to stretch the enjoyment over many months rather than a handful of days. Whenever a large deer is on the menu, my first thoughts are of .338 WMs.

I am a firm believer that the .338 is the most effective and broadly useful medium-bore caliber ever designed. That said, for this hunt I would surely rely on my favorite rifle. It is custom built on an FN Mauser action and carries a Bohler special steel barrel. The scope is a Kahles CB 2.5-10x50mm illuminated model with a custom stock turned from a marvelous piece of high-figure walnut. With this rifle, I shoot a custom load designed for me by Superior Ammunition. The load pushes a 250-grain Sierra Game King along at a smart 2,725 fps. This ballistic combination drops everything from coyotes to moose with equal aplomb.

Finally, after months of planning and waiting, departure day arrived. The nine-hour overnight flight brought us to Budapest early the next morning. Having cleared customs, we were met by Toni Török, Beretta's local hunting agent and Peter's partner. Three hours on Hungary's excellent highway system—a leftover vestige of Cold War Soviet influence—brought us to our final destination: the simple, comfortable Csöprönd lodge.

We took a few minutes to unpack our basic necessities and were led outside to meet our guides. The guides in Europe are called hunters or jaegers, and their skill and professionalism are similar to African professional hunters. Intense game management dictates that all hunts are fully guided and conducted one on one. The hunter is in command of the party, and you must follow his or her instructions to the letter. My hunter was Alexi, who goes by Alex. He spoke little English, and I speak no Hungarian. Luckily, the semiofficial language of European hunting is German. I know enough basic hunting words that, when combined with rudimentary sign language, Alex and I were confident we could communicate adequately.

Alex and I loaded into his truck and headed out. A short drive from the lodge, we came to an old logging road cut into the timber. As we walked the path, a heavy mist descended. About a half-mile down the trail, a large pasture appeared before us. Heavily coated in an ever-denser fog, the pasture acquired a distinct mystical quality. It was then that I heard for the first time the distinct roar of a stag searching for a mate. Aptly called a roar, the sound is more like that of a big lion informing you of his dominance, not something you would expect to hear from a member of the deer family. The cadence and volume are similar to an elk's bugle, but the tone is entirely unique. Where an elk's cry is a hoarse whistle, the stag's roar is deep, throaty, and full of rasp. The tone and rattle can give the hunter a good indication of maturity. The insistent calling of a stag in season affords the hunter an unusual and exciting tactic. In addition to spot and stalk, a hunter can use listen and stalk with a good chance of success.

Knowing generally where the stag was gave us the opportunity to set up prior to his arrival. Edging our way along the timberline, we came to one of Europe's distinct high seats. These simple yet quite comfortable stands are commonly seen in the hunting fields of Europe.

The results of five successful hunts displayed back at the lodge.

We scurried up the ladder, inserted the wide board seat, and readied ourselves for the arrival of the stag. For what seemed like an eternity, we heard him continue to roar from the far side of the pasture. Visibility was severely reduced by the fog, so the roaring stag easily stayed out of visual range. Finally, like the lady of the lake, one of his hinds, or female red deer, emerged from the mist. Her appearance brought my pulse up considerably. More hinds appeared. Still, the stag roared from beyond the wall of mist.

So sudden was his appearance that I thought I might be imagining him. His heavy and dark antlers rose high and wide. When he let out a roar, he reached forward with his neck and threw back his head, so his antlers nearly touched his back. Although the red stag is a generic twin to the American wapiti, the red deer has a few clear differences. The most renowned of these are the distinct crowns that top his antlers. They are a collection of three or more points that vary in configuration but are consistent in impact. The crowns give the stag his undeniably regal quality, a true majesty of appearance that washes over the observer like a waterfall.

When I saw the beautiful rack on this stag that swept high above his head, I quickly reached for my rifle. Without speaking, Alex grabbed my arm and shook his head in the negative. Dumbfounded, I looked at him questioningly. "Younger," he said. After he repeated it several times for me, I got the message. This stag was not yet mature and we would, therefore, not be taking him. Like any quality management program, the European one is focused on allowing each quality animal to reach its full potential. The pressure off, my pulse slowed, and I was able to enjoy the scene. For nearly a half an hour, we watched the stag roar and work his harem. Eventually, with the same angelic grace of their arrival, they made their exit. I had been in Hungary for about ten hours, and I already had a memory that would last a lifetime.

The next evening, two other hunters in camp, one of which was my father, were successful. My father, Martin, had taken a nice stag with his Franz Sodia double rifle, which was also chambered in .338 WM. The second barrel was nice to have, but by all accounts, it was not needed. Martin and his guide, Tamás, returned to camp with triumph evident on their faces. Martin's hatband bore the signature of a successful hunter in Europe, a branch dipped in the blood of the animal. This is worn back to the lodge as a sign of success. In addition, a piece of immediately available forage will always be fed to the fallen quarry. This provision of the final meal is another sign of care and respect for the game. The next morning the jag antlers, or hunting antlers, were played. The jaegers play songs that honor both the hunter and the fallen game. These are three of the many hunting rituals that are unique to Europe, and they add a great deal of flavor to the hunt.

After the late morning playing of the jag antlers, Alex and I returned to the field. We headed to a forest area known for quality stag. We walked a grass-covered logging trail. The woods to our left opened up into a large pasture of wild grass and small scrub trees. In the forest to our right, we heard a few distinct roars. Encouraged that the area was active, we continued to make our way along the path.

About a mile into our walk, we heard from the forest a powerful roar that was quickly answered by another deeper response. Quickly, Alex and I made our way to a high seat conveniently located at the intersection of two logging roads about fifty yards from our current location. We hoped the stag or stags would cross one of the two logging paths and offer us a shot.

Before we reached the top of the ladder, the powerful antler on antler crash of a fight in progress reached my ears. Although not yet in view, those stags were close at hand, and they were clearly mature stags to be fighting with such vigor. Subconsciously, I kept leaning further and further forward in hopes of seeing one of the knights doing battle in the forest. In a flash, a stag crossed the trail. I could tell it had antlers, but at the speed he was moving not much else was apparent. As if taunting us, he crossed back over in a single leap. Alex motioned for me to get my rifle ready. We had a shootable stag in the area.

I steeled myself for a quick shot. The roaring of their voices and crashing of their antlers seemed to be right on top of us, yet we could not see them. A small rise was blocking them from view. As darkness descended and my frustration was mounting, I heard another roar. This one was the deepest, grainiest, and loudest I had heard since my arrival. It was coming from behind us. I turned and looked over my left shoulder. There in the pasture stood a stag so large that he did not seem to be of the same breed as the others. His rack was tall, heavy, wide, and festooned with points. My jaw dropped, and my pulse quickened. After glancing at the stag, Alex hoarsely whispered, "Can shisen," meaning "Can shoot." I did not need to be told twice. I ranged the stag with my Leica Geovid 8x42 while he was quartering toward me at 227 yards. Knowing that range was not an issue, I slowly brought my rifle into battery. I put the crosshairs directly on the point of his shoulder and squeezed the trigger. The 250-grain slug hit with an audible wonk and the stag sat down in place. His back end gave out first as he landed in his tracks. Excitement got the better of my Euro-sensitive sensibilities, and I let out a victory whoop. Surprisingly, Alex responded with a stiff high five.

We climbed down from the stand and made our way to the downed monarch. Upon closer review, he was bigger than I had imagined. Not only tall and wide, his antlers were incredibly heavy. My hands were unable to close around the main beam at its highest point. Alex fed the stag his last meal, then handed me a bloodied branch. Proudly, I secured it to my hat and took a couple of quick photos as darkness began to develop around us.

Dad Martin Parker and a nice stag taken with a double rifle.

That evening, Gyula "Julius" Varga, a local game official whom I befriended on a prior Hungarian hunt, stopped by the lodge to visit. Upon seeing my stag, he remarked that it was surely a high gold-medal animal and would likely be one of the best stags taken in Hungary that year. He estimated his age at thirteen or fourteen years. Later, when the skull and antlers were weighed at 11.3 kilos, he reached high into the gold-medal class.

Julius taught me a German phrase that is used to describe such a trophy, "lebens hirsch." This means "the stag of your life." The phrase came to me as yet another interesting part of a distinctively European hunt.

In the next several days, I took a fine wild boar, and my father took another stag and a mouflon ram. We laughed, worked, and hunted together. I don't know how to say the hunt of your life in German, but if I did, I would. I had seen a beautiful country, been in the best stag area in the world, shared a camp with my favorite hunting partner, and taken the stag of my life. How could it have been better?

Chapter Nineteen

The World of Beretta

Hungary is known throughout the international hunting community for consistently producing the most medal-class roebucks each year. Those who hunt it are proud of this and protective of the fact. It is an odd dichotomy, because you naturally want to share this place with people who will appreciate the traditions and cultures and game, yet you want to protect the places. Such are the nuances of so many conversations amongst hunters at the Safari Club International gatherings. A brief talk at an SCI Convention in Reno with Chris Dorsey, the renowned hunting show host, inevitably involved the topic of good roebuck hunting. This little buck is one of the most sought-after animals in the international hunting community. This trophy is a sign amongst hunters that needs no explanation. Chris and I had previously discussed organizing an Eastern European hunt several times, but this time I told him I was ready to share my little Hungarian deer world that would quickly show, like on a treasure map, where X marks the spot. Dorsey quickly digested this fact and had one question. "When do we go?"

We were soon airborne on Delta flight 98, which took us directly from New York to Budapest. Upon arrival, we were met by my partner Toni Török and Chris. Jesse Johnson, a videographer who would film this hunt, and I piled into our Mercedes van, along with an expedition's worth of camera equipment, Beretta clothing for the guides, Sako and Tikka rifles, and lots of personal stuff. After a scenic three-hour drive, we arrived at the hunting lodge of my old friend Miklós Támba, which was near Napkor in Eastern Hungary. Miklós served us lunch, then sent the group upstairs for a well-deserved nap that allowed us to reset ourselves before we headed out to sight our rifles. There were interviews before dinner. Chris and Jesse reviewed the video details. Toni and I worked on how to place Jesse in the right place at the right time, so he could capture the shot on film.

The first morning, we brought in a beautiful carriage with a magnificent pair of midnight black horses to give Chris and Jesse the feeling of how aristocrats and nobles hunted my favorite little buck more than one hundred twenty years ago in the Golden Age before the start of the twentieth century—before Europe was changed by two world wars. Toni

Now this is what I call a sweet ride.

and I headed off with Jozsef, our guide, into the forest to stalk a prized buck that was previously spotted. Let me tell you, this was one smart old buck. We would sneak up on him from the bottom of a hill, and he would cleverly sneak to the other side. We would move our position to where we thought he should have been only to realize he had quietly moved back again. This song and dance went on for a couple of hours before we threw in our hats. The old boy had won the game.

As we continued our leisurely walk through the woods, we observed one or two females, or suta; some small bucks, or kicsi; and a few males still in velvet, or barkas; but no good bucks, or jobak. All hunters learn these four Hungarian words quickly, and your heart rate learns them, too. Hopes rise as one approaches each little buck of Puszta, but they return to normal if the word is not a jobak. We now agreed to see what we could find by climbing into a high seat. One fox and one hare later, we descended and continued walking, which was prudent, as the woods and fields are magical in this part of Eastern Hungary. They hold huge amounts of roe deer. The first morning I counted twenty bucks of all sizes and twenty-nine bucks on the second morning, which always makes me wonder—if I saw forty-nine bucks in the forest, how many bucks did I pass and not see?

By our evening rendezvous, I learned Chris had his second buck, a bronze medal, to go with his silver from the first day. Jesse captured both on video, an accomplishment at least as difficult as placing a good shot. When hunting roebuck, you are stalking in the forest. You must forget, or try to forget, that a camera is following in your footsteps. You must stay focused on the stalk and try not to think about the second hunter, who is armed with a camera. You must stay focused and trust the cameraman to be so skilled as to find the right spot and start filming at the right time. It is a wonder to behold and be a part of. I rarely realized that I was actually being filmed, which is a testament to Chris's skill at stalking a hunter stalking an animal and capturing two moments at once on film.

Chris also proved to be a fun hunter. His first buck was spotted by his guide, Attila, about a half-mile away. There was a tree line most of the way—except for the first two hundred yards or so. The lack of cover did not matter. Chris smoothly zeroed in on the big boy with his Tikka T3. His second buck encounter came in the deep woods. After playing the Hungarian word game with no mention of a jobak, Chris saw a deer feeding in the distance. His eyes can locate game as well as any guide. Upon closer inspection, he turned out to be a nice old male who was at least eight years old with trophy-sized antlers sitting regally atop his head. After much discussion, mostly in sign language, our small group decided to climb a high ridge and view the buck from above. Noticing that the deer was facing the opposite direction while feeding, Chris proceeded slowly and placed one foot in front of the other until he was in shooting range. A medal-class buck was secured.

It was now my third morning hunting with my buddy Karcsi. We saw a monster deer fly by as soon as we reached our hunting destination. This was a good sign—bucks were on the move. Now that Chris's part of the hunt was over, he joined me for mine and enthusiastically volunteered another set of eyes.

Driving along the numerous hedgerows, we counted approximately fifty deer of all shapes, sizes, and sexes, which is not uncommon for a single day in Eastern Hungary. As we entered the cool forest, the bark from a buck deep within the woods welcomed our group. We allowed the truck to roll to a complete stop and listened for a sign to tell us in which direction to begin the stalk. The only problem with so many deer roaming everywhere is the number standing as lookouts that can give away your presence. For the first fifteen minutes or so, we followed a dirt road to guide us toward glory. But then we found ourselves in the thickest of woods.

Spotting something beige up ahead proved to be a lone suta that we managed to luckily sneak around, as a handy ravine let us pass by unnoticed. After trekking down a steep hill and up a slight incline, Chris pointed in the direction of a feeding roebuck. Karcsi confirmed my call that it was indeed a jobak. I moved to a big tree that provided excellent camouflage. Chris came with me. I positioned my Sako against the tree. The buck moved a bit forward. Chris wanted to know if I could see his breadbasket, which was where I was already focusing my Burris 2X12 scope. I calmly whispered, "I got him. I am right on his chest."

Karcsi was now very excited. "Shoot! Shoot! Shoot!" he enthusiastically repeated several times. I never felt the gun go off. I knew it was a solid hit. The others confirmed the same with the help of their binoculars. We tracked the buck for about fifty or sixty yards. He was lying in the bushes. Let me tell you, shooting with cameras focused on you makes the stakes much higher. I was happy with my good buck. He was confirmed as a bronze medal, but I was even more elated that the event was over. I really admire Chris for shooting on camera again and again.

I savored my 152nd roebuck. Yes, I have a bit of a thing for little deer, just as this jobak would be enjoyed by millions of fellow hunters for years to come through the magic of television.

Hunger set in as we finished preparing the buck for the larder. Coffee and toast was all we had eaten since 4 a.m. It was now almost 10 a.m., and we were starving. Karcsi's wife, Erika, understands hunters, and she had one of those "light" Hungarian breakfasts on the table ready for our merry band of hunters. We were in a hunter's house. At Karcsi's home, Chris and Jesse saw numerous trophies that belonged to the master of the house. Stag. Roebuck. Boar. Fallow deer. Mouflon. Ibex. Chamois. Capercaillie. Wolf. It was good to be there amongst brother hunters before day turned into night.

We returned to Budapest early the next morning to my base camp, Le Meridien Hotel, which provided a more urbane counterbalance to Karcsi's hunting lodge. We taped our final interview at a hunting area near Budapest. We filmed some super trophies, such as former head of

The ever-present wines of Tokaj.

the Soviet Union Leonid Brezhnev's sixteen-point stag and a collection of Pal Csergezan paintings. Csergezan is the David Sheppard and Bob Kuhn of European game rolled into one. Then, out of nowhere, Toni presented me with the Order of St. Hubertus. He told me I was the first American to receive this award. I was stunned. I didn't know why I was receiving such a high honor amongst hunters. Toni said it had been decided by the committee that I would be inducted into the Order in recognition of my twenty-five years of service to Hungary, developing hunting and tourism with Americans and the many certifications given by Hungarian hunters that I had displayed qualities they admired in a sportsman. In addition, they were appreciative of all the articles I had written about the country. I was humbled. Even now, the plaque occupies a special place of honor in my office at the Beretta Gallery in Manhattan. The medal of the Order of St. Hubertus is in my trophy room. I wear the Order's lapel pin with the greatest pride. Toni informed me that normally, there is a serious ceremony and dinner that follows with this honor, but the TV show interfered.

I was not bothered in the least. I was ecstatic and honored to even have received the award. Soon, I would be flying across the Atlantic Ocean back to New York, but already I was making the final plans for the next excursion into the heart of what once had been the Austro-Hungarian Empire. I couldn't wait to return to a land where time seems to stand still, and all that is best ages like some exquisite painting, which reveals more of itself the more time one spends studying the canvas.

Steve Weiss in the same area several years before with a guide and a gold-medal roebuck.

Chapter Twenty

Winning Over a Wily Buck

Seasons are always an important consideration when hunting roebuck in Hungary, but it is a fact that these feisty little deer provide a worthy challenge no matter the time of year. The best roebuck trophy hunting the world has to offer is here in Hungary amidst the former Austro-Hungarian Empire. The tradition dates back more than one hundred fifty years, when nobles hunted roe deer every day except Sunday. This wily little buck has long been considered royal game, and it holds court with other sought-after animals, such as the red stag, wild boar, and fallow deer. Even today, you can hunt roebuck from a horse-drawn carriage pulled by a famed pair of Hungarian Nonius horses, as counts and barons did in the days of old.

A hunter's dozen.

With my new Beretta Mato rifle in .270 Winchester and Federal 130-grain Nosler ballistic tip ammunition, I was ready for this adventure. We planned the trip for mid-July even though we knew July is one of the most difficult times of the year to hunt, even in game-rich Hungary. The sun pushes the temperature toward 100 degrees. Mosquitoes are out in full force, and everything reminds me of Africa—my beloved Africa.

Yet we were back. It was 3:30 a.m. Toni, Dr. Marinos Petratos, and I were in the thick of our familiar routine. It was dark. The moon was still out. We were leaving a hunting lodge. We had a half-hour ride, then a twenty-minute walk to our stands, where we would settle and wait while the cool morning breeze awakened our senses. At 4:30 a.m., the breezes are always cool, and daybreak fools you into a false sense of hope that the day will prove comfortable.

It is always a good thing to see game early. It serves as a mental counterbalance to what lies ahead for you. Before the sun rose above the horizon, a nice buck answered our doe call. I thought the rut must be on, so I let this above-average buck melt back into the morning forest, only to later learn that the rut was not on. In fact, nothing was on, and nothing would soon move in the rising heat. It was clear that Marinos and I were in for a truly tough hunt.

There are four seasons to hunt roebuck. The best time is the middle of April to the middle of May, when neither crops nor vegetation are high enough to swallow up the diminutive deer. When the season opens in April, a dedicated hunter can expect to see twelve to twenty quality bucks per day. Two years ago, I saw seventeen good heads in a single morning of easy stalking and carriage riding.

The second hunting period takes place May 16 through July 25. This is the most difficult time to hunt because of the lush forest undergrowth, the height and density of crops, and meadows conceal game from the eyes of hunters. Naturally, Marinos and I were ready to try our luck. It was his fourth trip and my thirty-first, and neither of us had hunted in Hungary this time of year.

The third time frame for the roebuck is July 25 through August 10 during the rut. Watching deer at this time of year shows hunters how determined the male is as a suitor. With equal vigor, bucks will track down the call of a doe in heat or the plaintive cry of a fawn calling to

Peter and Toni with two of the author's gold-medal roebucks.

its mother. The boys are aggressive at this time of year. They will fight to the death if their territories are threatened. Roebucks with straight antlers are known as killer bucks, as their dagger-like antlers can easily puncture a lung or an eye during an encounter with another of its kind. You can hunt roe all day this time of year by hiding in a good thicket or sitting in a stand using a first-class call. Just remember to watch for the direction of the wind and know your game's territory.

The final season is September 1 through September 30. During the magnificent roaring of the red stags, I have often encountered good roebucks in the woods that have developed a false sense of security. At this time of year, roe licenses are few, but with some luck one may find its way to you.

After a few days of hunting in the immediate area known for exceptional roe deer, Marinos and I managed three average bucks. During the end of July, when the heat level is high and the rut hasn't yet started, there is no choosing. You take what you happen upon. Without the rut, chance and luck are your best friends.

Of Latitudes and Longitudes

Though one can never do anything to influence the seasons, geography is malleable. Marinos and I moved to the Zemplen Mountains, near the border of Slovakia, for a little relief from the tropical weather. We reached the hunting lodge, a thick-walled structure built of old timbers and covered with exceptional trophies of past hunts. In the nearby forests, where it was much cooler, we stalked through some of the most spectacular scenery in Hungary. On our first morning out, the sound of

A home away from home.

a rock falling caught my attention. As I turned, a young boar ran full tilt across the trail. He scurried up the side of a steep hill about one hundred fifty yards from us. I aimed the Swarovski 2.5-10X scope on the pig's front third and let off a shot. The boar tumbled twenty yards down the hill, stopping dead at the trail's edge. This end result was preferable to tracking a wounded boar in thick bush. The combination of the .270 caliber Beretta Mato and 150-grain Federal ammunition got the job done well, as it is difficult to stop even a small boar in mid-run. As we made our way back to the lodge, Marinos walked in with another roebuck and a mouflon ewe.

Although we were having some success, the game was still not moving. Toni made some calls and discovered that the rut was just beginning in the Devecser area, not far from Lake Balaton. So, we moved again. Unlike other countries, Hungary offers hunters the chance to improve their luck, because many diverse hunting regions are within easy access of each other. Hungary is a little smaller than Indiana—about 15 percent smaller than England. The first night in our new area, we spotted a roebuck in the distance as we were dropping off the doctor for an evening stalk. Everyone froze. I handed Marinos the rifle. His guide let out a doe call, and a buck immediately bounded directly toward us like a lovesick puppy. When the buck stopped, the doctor was already in a kneeling position. His bullet found its mark.

The rut was on. Our luck was beginning to change. I was looking for a medal-class buck, which is much easier to come by in April than

July. Toni quickly informed me that older bucks are weary and do not always come into a call, even during the height of the rut. Like the whitetail deer, they don't get old by being stupid.

On our last night of the hunt, we approached a stand at about 7:30 p.m. A buck appeared within a few minutes after we settled into our blind. At first, it looked like an average deer. My guide, Imre, was staring extra hard through his 10X40 binoculars. With only the benefit of mediocre light, he gauged the buck's antlers to be about ten inches with a mature face and body, which meant the buck was six or seven years old, but the old boy's rack looked a tad thin. I lowered my Mato and grabbed my binoculars for yet another look. Just then, Imre must have seen the same thing I did. As the buck put its head down to graze, a large pair of bases with dark pearling was revealed. I quickly removed my 150-grain bullets—I was really looking for boar—and slipped in 130-grain ammo, which is something you do only after you know the different points of impact on an animal. The breeze died down and the sight picture was crystal clear. I squeezed the trigger. The crosshairs were on the buck's shoulder. A quick second shot put the deer down as he was in his death wobble. It was a heavy, seven-year-old record-class buck. "Perhaps the largest shot in the area this year," my guide declared.

It was wonderful to be in an area that, even at the worst time of the year, offers the chance to see an abundance of red deer, boar, roebuck, fallow deer, badger, fox, hare, and martin, all in just two days of hunting. If the weather were a bit cooler, hunting for roebuck during the rut could prove to be a real joy. Those who hunt often know weather, game, and luck are all things you cannot control.

As I have said numerous times, I would rather be lucky than good. Hunting roebuck opening day in April has no equal; in the right area, you can see a number of good bucks each and every day. In our areas in Eastern Hungary, I counted over 150 roe deer just driving around two days before the beginning of the season in 2006. Due to some of the most aggressive game management in Europe, coupled with expansive agricultural areas and a general respect for wild game, Hungary has maintained a healthy game population unparalleled anywhere else in Europe.

Hunting during the rut gives one the unique experience of watching the bucks respond to the wooden whistles used by the skilled Hungarian guides. In early fall, when the roaring of the stags splits the morning air wide open, you may happen upon a good roebuck. If after taking your stag, you find yourself with several days left over, you may take this time to hunt for a fine roebuck or big wild boar. So many times you come home with a totally unexpected trophy while hunting for another one.

With Lodovico Antinori, from whom the author has learned much about the roebuck.

I remember once hunting for stag with Steven Weiss and Marinos when the rut was not on. We never shot a stag, but we came home with three good boar and two mouflon. Also, while walking in from an unsuccessful boar hunt in Romania, I took a medal-class roebuck that was crossing out of a field not eighty meters away. My stag of a lifetime was taken while going for roebuck right after the demise of Nicolae Ceauşescu.

Whenever you decide to hunt roebuck in Hungary, know one thing: you are truly in the land of giants.

Chapter Twenty-One

The Perfect Walk-Up

"Uncle" Billie Schaefer and I came to Budapest a few days before one of the Beretta groups' driven pheasant and flighted duck weeks. We were invited by Zoltan, the region's head hunter, to shoot in a hunting block not far from the driven pheasant area. The game was to be wild pheasant, hare, and hopefully a duck or two! In this location, the birds are not bred. Many escape from driven areas and join their brethren in the wild. Any pheasant that have made it past the foxes, birds of prey, and guns are wild by any definition. These are tough birds, too. Their tails are long, and you definitely want to stay away from their spurs.

We had four guides, a Vizsla, and a German shorthair in our merry little band. It was a crisp November morning, cloudy with just the right amount of wind. With guns at the ready, Bill and I started off on either side of a large hedgerow that led to endless hectares of corn and wheat. Two guides and their dogs worked just in front of us while two other guides stationed themselves as stoppers at the end of the long row. After

Toni and Peter with hare.

a few minutes of walking slowly to let the dogs do their job, a cock bird flew out in fourth gear thirty yards in front of Bill. He brought it down nicely just outside the corn. As I turned to give him a "Well done," a hare appeared as if by magic from behind a small clump of old corn. I lifted my Beretta Jubilee and dispatched the harried hare. Now, whatever happened the rest of the day was pure bonus. We had already completed the menu. Bill, who is one of the finest game shots around, pulled ahead of a hen and cock bird and dropped them both within easy reach of the guide.

As we came to the last fifty yards of the four-hundred-yard hedge, the two men at the end began acting as beaters. The one guide who spoke German told me there were a lot of birds all running towards the end. Billie and I spread out about twenty-five yards into the surrounding fields. Then it started! As the dogs moved forward and the guides at the end entered the hedge, the birds began to fly everywhere trying to escape. We could not load fast enough. We took down seven more pheasant, missing the two easiest ones. When we finally reached the end of the hedge thinking the hunt was over, a hare burst out in between two of the guides. I had to let him run out into the field before attempting a safe shot. With a clear miss behind the hopper using the first barrel, I sent him to hare heaven with the second. The bag for the first hedgerow—and we weren't even in the good shooting area—was eleven pheasants and three hare.

Our next chance at a few birds was in a huge cornfield. Working each row ever so slowly, we were able to put up many birds and connected on a couple more hare attempting to leave the county. In between the two fields was a large drainage ditch situated near the farm road. The guide informed us a lot of birds like to hide down there. We positioned ourselves on either side of the ditch and motioned for the two guides to stand at the end. After the dogs were sent in, it wasn't thirty seconds before Bill hit a hare and I smoked a left and a right on a pair of cock birds. We worked deliberately. These birds had not been hunted since last year. They felt safe in their hideaway.

Suddenly, the young Vizsla, who had been flawless up until then, began bumping a lot of birds. The guide whistled her back to him and proceeded to kick the dog for her transgression. Well, Bill and I freaked out. Bill and Barbara Schaefer have three English setters, and my old buddy Yellow Brooks Hi-Brass, a German shorthair, were like family to us, so this didn't sit well. I demanded that the head guide, whom I've known for ten years or so, tell the young lad that I would personally kick him the same way, only harder, if he kicked the dog again.

The guide, who shall go nameless, later apologized profusely. He said he was trying to make the dog work well for the famous American hunters.

I replied, "If you continue to treat this fine animal in this way, you will lose a potentially super hunting dog." Years later, the same

Two intent members of the hunt.

guide took me out alone on a walk-up with this incredible dog, which had now developed into a field champion. The dog was a thing of beauty to watch. I felt a gleam of pride, thinking perhaps my harsh words helped this young handler become more understanding about the correct way to teach a dog to hunt.

Now, we approached a cornfield that had already been cut. A hare broke to Bill's right, and at the same time, one jumped out to my left. It took all four shots, but we had a combined double. This field seemed to be saturated with hare. They were all sunning themselves in the late morning sun. With a successful start to the day under our belt, we headed to an old farmhouse where a wonderful lunch was ready and waiting on the table for our team. Goulash soup was our first dish, then roast chicken and pork, five kinds of vegetables, and salad rounded out the meal. All of this was topped off with some homemade bread, cake, strong coffee, and a couple of Cuban cigars. We were good to go.

The sun came out a bit brighter in the short fall afternoon. We now worked our way into another area where the hare loved to sun themselves. As we exited a hedgerow, an unexpected pheasant made his getaway. Not even one safety came off. I guess the bird got the edge

One of my favorite walk-up partners, Sylvia Rafford, and her wonderful Beretta 687EELL.

on us due to the lingering effects of an overindulgent lunch and a joke Bill was attempting to translate. A huge roebuck burst from the trees not fifty yards from us while we had a good laugh over our missed opportunity; on his head stood four-hundred-plus grams of perfectly formed antlers. I followed him with my 12-gauge, thinking how fortunate he was that it was November. This distraction was short-lived as we began to walk into the field. I saw one, then two, then a dozen hare lingering outside the hedgerow. Looking further ahead, we spotted a dozen more oversized bunnies. I yelled at Bill to keep his gun loaded. The shooting could become fast and furious. We made two nice shots on a couple of hare trying to make a dash for the hedgerow. These animals do not wait for the dogs to get close. You must be prepared for long shots anytime you glimpse long ears. The same is true when the pointer gets birdie.

The body language of a good hunting dog always helps you be more prepared for when the pheasant explodes into the air. As the dog's tail begins moving and his head goes down, it is a giveaway that a bird is near or has recently walked by. This is when I keep a close watch on my canine friend. Now, our pup was getting excited. He continued to make smaller and smaller circles and finished with a dead stop.

He seemed to almost fall over as he locked up on a wily old cock bird trying to conceal himself in a place where nothing could hide.

Just as I hollered to Bill telling him where the bird was, a hen shot out in the opposite direction. The cock bird thought this was an excellent time to make his escape. Bill was already on the hen, and I never looked away from my bird. We had another nice team pair, and as the sun began giving way to the cold of early evening, a large flight of mallards came directly overhead. With one more sweep of the Beretta paintbrush, we felled four ducks at once. The total bag for the day were forty-nine pheasants, two dozen hare, and four ducks, which we tied to the side of our big trailer pulled by an old Russian tractor. It was a good day.

I have done a number of walk-ups since this one and most likely have a few more to go, but I will always remember this day with Bill as the most perfect walk-up. We had the flawless combination of good dogs, good shooting, good game, and good friends.

The results of a four-gun walk-up.

Chapter Twenty-Two

The Stag Rut Around Lábod

If you walk down Madison Avenue and you did not know where to find the Beretta Gallery, you might walk right past the window front that looks like any other Madison Avenue boutique. You would never realize you were standing before one of the world's great gun rooms, several floors of top-notch kit, and items from our hunting past, such as Ernest Hemingway's SO3 Beretta shotgun. When I am in the States and not in Hungary, Romania, or on a journey to some other distant hunting ground, I spend my time in a study high above this 63rd Street townhouse that we have occupied ever since we opened the Beretta Gallery in 1995. The beauty of an office in a place such as this is that it attracts endless hunters. I would say the Beretta Gallery is to globe-trotting hunters as Grand Central Station is to train travel. We always seem to be busy as many old friends and some of newer vintages regularly stop by to say hello and visit. I well remember when Michael Groom and his girlfriend Chris Moore arrived in New York in September 2008 for a few days before our planned journey to Budapest. They stopped by the Beretta Gallery to buy clothing and kits for the stag hunt and their November driven pheasant shoot we would soon leave for.

These trips tend to be like family affairs; I am lucky Debbie shares my passion for the hunt. She and I had dinner with Michael and Chris that night. These dinners with our hunters inevitably resemble intelligence debriefings. Debbie is an experienced Hungarian stag hunter. She and I explain all the details of the hunt. Debbie, whose expertise in the

Make my day!

field extends into the city, knows the best places to shop in Budapest. Listening to Debbie talk of the hunt with Chris and Michael got me excited. Yes, even after dozens of stag hunts, I still get excited. My pulse still quickens at the mention of hunting the same way it did when I was a boy and spent so many days in the fields and woods in upstate New York with just a rifle and some ammo. I wished the day would never end and my life would be one long perpetual hunt. I have learned that those feelings—those memories of childhood—are the same with many people. That is why I am always especially happy to reunite with my friends and partners in Hungary.

On this stag hunt with Michael and Chris, we were naturally with my partner, Toni, whose love and passion for the hunt rivals mine. Lodovico Antinori and Karl Grund, the renowned gun maker from Ferlach, Austria, also joined us. In truth, I needed this particular trip as much as anyone—maybe even more. I find that sometimes I need to step away from the gravitational pull of adult life, which at that time involved preparing guns for a museum display on Ernest Hemingway, making sure the first two Beretta SO10 EELL shotguns and part of the set of five made to commemorate one hunter's five favorite hunting dogs arrived on time, and also attending to real estate. Debbie and I were trying to sell a house in Connecticut while buying one in

Westchester County, New York (with a super trophy room, by the way). I needed to be among the morning mist, the roaring of the stags, and the smell of the rut. They are burned in my memory. They are indelible, and they call me back, like they call all hunters.

For me, and I know I am not alone, hunting continually brings me new experiences, and it continually creates memories—it is a storybook. Each year has different trips, and some parts of the year are particularly special because I get to see old friends or old places on favorite hunts.

I also take solace in the little quiet rituals of the hunt, such as waking when it is still night and dressing while half asleep, only to be refreshed by the cool morning air and smell of a wood fire. It makes my adrenaline flow. The excitement for me is the same today as it was for me when I began hunting more than fifty years ago and first took some of my most memorable trophies, including my first bongo, elephant, and brown bear, and even my first whitetail deer. When the excitement disappears, when you no longer take pleasure from the totality of the hunt, you must stop hunting. When you are still filled with excitement, you must hunt.

So I find myself returning to Budapest, landing at the airport, and driving into the countryside. Besides, you never know whom you will meet. A familiar face smiled at me and said hello as Chris, Michael, and I stepped outside Budapest's Ferenc Liszt International Airport. It was not my partner, Toni, but Peter, my old Hungarian friend from Manhattan's Post House restaurant, who has waited on my family and a plethora of famous and infamous hunters from every corner of the world for more than fifteen years. Soon, we made the scenic ride to our hunting grounds in Lábod. We arrived to 85 degree weather. Karl, his wife Renata, and their daughter Diana were already there. After a quick shower and a tasty lunch, we sighted in our rifles at one hundred twenty yards. Michael's shot was an inch high right above the X, and mine was the same but a half-inch to the left. We now split up into two groups. Michael and Chris would form one group with Tamás as their guide, and Toni and I would make up the second group with another guide also named Tamás.

Before heading into the fields, we spent a good half-hour admiring Karl's sixteen-point, 11.3-kilo gold-medal stag taken earlier in the morning, which was hanging inside a cool room. We left the Vadászház, or hunting house, for a half-hour ride through the thick forest and occasional fields of corn that broke up an otherwise continuous tree line. Even though it was still hot at 6 p.m., we saw three hinds and a small boar. After a bit more traveling over bumpy roads, we hit a large open field of two hundred fifty acres, about a quarter of which was planted with corn. There were no fewer than five stands in the area. We walked down the road just outside the corn. We climbed up to our high seat. I felt comfortable. The stand was much the same as the hundreds I have managed to ascend over the years. I quickly found my best shooting position. I took out my soft seat and put my polar fleece in front of me as a rest. Next, I discussed with Tamás about how to best manage a shot from all 360 degrees of the stand. Feeling slightly apprehensive, Toni and Tamás decided we should move forward to another stand in the middle of the corn to increase our view. Almost immediately, we heard stags roar.

First, we saw a small roebuck, then two young stags, a hind, a fox, and three more hinds. The big boys stayed in the other field or in the safety of the forest until it was too dark for a shot. We counted ten stags in all by the time we climbed down from the stand at 8:20 p.m. As we now knew where the stags were hanging out, we knew where to try our luck early the next day. We would leave the lodge at 4:15 a.m. sharp. This would be our routine every day until hopefully St. Hubertus blessed us with success.

Hunting is often a solitary pursuit, but I am always quietly amazed because successful hunting is sometimes a group effort. Every hunting lodge, like every hunting party, functions like a spy network. One morning, Michael watched two hinds, followed by an 8.5-kilo stag that stood in the open at seventy-five yards. He let that bad boy walk on by.

At dinner that night, we all knew the animals were moving, and we were in the right place at the right time. Cold beer and a super dinner do much to enhance the end-of-day stories from the field and hasten sleep. Sometimes, the alarm clock never sounds—at least not the alarm clock that was set. That morning at 4 a.m., I heard my first stag of the day, which I took as a good omen and a reminder that I was indeed back in the hunt. All those worldly cares—such as selling houses, dealing with the office, and the intricacies of guns and museums—were on the other side of the world. All that mattered now was outside the Vadászház.

The always welcome pot of Hungarian goulash.

Stalking

We stalked deer for about an hour after hearing three stags out for their early morning roar. After deciding on a shooting lane just inside a small forest and across from a big cornfield, we spotted four small stags, four hinds, one fallow deer, two roebucks, and a fox. We saw this between 6:30 and 7:20 a.m. We next heard six stags roar. The nearest stag was two hundred yards away, but he sounded young so he received safe passage. We heard a distant stag with an extremely low roar that only comes from really old boys. At breakfast, during Michael's morning report, he mentioned they had seen the same 8.5-kilo stag from the night before bedded down at one hundred thirty yards. "If only I could take a second deer," he said, "I would have shot that one in a heartbeat." Michael now had permission to take a second red deer, and our fingers were crossed that he would be successful later that day.

Tamás and I took the Grunds, Chris, and Michael to see Lábod's hunting lodges and have lunch in the dining hall of a smaller lodge. After a quick nap, back we went to our stands of choice.

Tamás, Toni, and I headed to the same area where we heard all of those stags roaring the night before. As we approached the blind, a wild cat and a nice roebuck made their presence known. I thought our luck was about to change. I eased myself into the stand. I checked my shooting positions. I tested my Burris 2x10 red dot scope, making sure of the finest clarity. Stand shooting can be extremely easy or extremely hard depending on where your quarry appears. It is your duty to think of every possibility beforehand. You definitely do not want to be banging the rifle or yourself around at the pivotal moment.

If you want results like this, use enough gun like Rich Clark did.

A Roar and a Bang

The stags began to roar. Amongst the six we heard, we knew two were old boys and one was a young fella we called Boy George, who had a shallow roar that occasionally sounded like a high-pitched squeal. When you cannot see stags and thus cannot judge their antlers, the key information about the quality of the trophy is their roar. The tenor of the roar tells if the stag is an old boy or a Boy George. There is nothing quite like the sound of a senior stag roaring within one hundred fifty yards of you in an otherwise silent forest. You will never forget watching a gold-medal stag go into a face-contorting roar to break the morning's peace.

While we waited in the stand, the wild cat resurfaced again, along with two roebucks, a young stag, and finally two hinds from the left and eight from the right, where we heard the deepest roaring. The night was dark, but just a quarter of the moon peeking in and out of the clouds provided enough light. We could make out some black spots as ladies. I am sure this was part of the boss's harem and that he would show up in the total blackness a few minutes later. This is when you stretch and start thinking of the wonderful dinner you so richly deserve for coming home, yet again, empty-handed.

The rain began early the next morning and continued on and off for a few hours. We spotted a hawk. We saw one hind and one undersized deer by 5:20 a.m. Michael saw two stags, one more than seven kilos, but they were too young to take. Karl saw another young stag. Considering it was raining hard for half of the morning, we saw quite a lot of game.

I was sitting by the rifle range under a shaded tree discussing upcoming shoots and hunts during the next three months with Toni. A cool breeze finally assaulted the unbearable heat of the first two days. Perhaps my luck was about to change, as with the cold comes the stag.

Our new morning brought us to a stand just inside a tree line, where we had seen a stag and a bunch of females the night before. The rain stopped by 10 a.m. and the forest came alive. We kept seeing animals all during our drive and stalk into our designated area.

Michael had passed on yet another decent stag. He was still holding out for a real trophy. Karl managed a cull stag that needed to be taken out of the gene pool. The same reports came from everyone. They were seeing stag, but they were all too small.

It was going to be my morning—or so I thought. As we left the truck by the side of the road, I heard a stag almost immediately. It was that low, deep roar I had been waiting for. After a slow creep through pitch-black woods, we located our stand facing a one hundred by six hundred yard open hay field.

The early morning stand.

The old boy was standing just inside the tree line, about two hundred yards in the distance. Joining the old boy's chorus was another big male to his right and a younger deer to his left. This has to be our morning, I told myself, as I eased up the ladder with my bad knee. Alas, the stag moved a bit closer before following the direction of the young kid. We scurried back down the ladder, traveled through the woods to the road, and headed down a trail at a mad pace, attempting to get ahead of the deer. We were successful. The stag was still singing, thereby giving his position away. We found a new stand. We once again climbed in. The stag was definitely coming our way. Now, the million-dollar question was if he would decide to rest in the forest in front of us or make the fatal mistake of crossing the opening to the woods, which was located to our side.

First, a couple of roebucks crossed in front of us; then we spotted the rear end of a stag (not our boy) sneak past. We continued to hear our intended victim. He was moving in our direction. Two females slowly moved through the trees. I was now ready at two hundred yards with my gun pointed in the direction of the open field within the deep woods. A stag nose appeared. Safety off. Ready to rumble. When he came into full view, his antlers were four to four-and-a-half kilos. I remember asking myself where the other half of his rack was. I had the scope on him for five to six seconds as he quietly disappeared into the other side of the forest. I took this as good news. He was going the way of all the other game we had seen. As the story goes, our stag stopped roaring and decided to check into a rest area on the wrong side of the tracks. As night fell, we set up in the field from where he came and hoped to catch him on his journey back to the cornfields.

Patterns

I was now recognizing paths and fields. I could pick out stands across the way that we were sitting in during our last foray. Yes, there it was yet again, the roaring similar to our last encounter. We dropped Toni off first to scout another field and report any action. We slowly made our way through the woods. We kept trying to figure in which opening in the forest the stag would make his appearance. We heard another two stags go off. We headed toward a stand at the end of the field that we had used that morning. We felt we were narrowing down on the old boy. It was like a good chess game.

The old boy was indeed getting closer, but at one hundred fifty yards or so, the brute turned toward another field. A couple of roebucks, five hinds, and a fox were spotted. It was now 8:20 p.m., and even with a half-moon, it was too dark for a shot. A stag sauntered out at nine hundred yards and neared four hundred yards to stop and laugh at us. The night was done, but the hunt was not over.

Now I was in the mid-hunt drill. Up at 4:15 a.m. Out at 5 a.m. Back by 9 a.m. for breakfast and a nap. Lunch at 2 p.m. Out again at 5 p.m. Back by 9 p.m. for dinner and bed by 10:30 p.m. After you repeat the routine for four or five days, you fall into a trance and wait for something to change.

We now had Lodovico's stories to add to our own, but tomorrow was yet another day. Perhaps it would be the day of the hunter. Out again at 5 a.m. full of the faithful hope of hunters that today was the day.

We rode to the area of the big stag, the one that was always one step ahead. Once again, we listened to him and three friends making a ruckus. It sounded as though one stag was in the field and another was just inside the woods. We stalked accordingly.

As we stood in the woods between the two stags, we made choices based on the wind, proximity, and tone of the roaring. We moved, he moved. He was always just ahead of us somewhere in the thickest part of the forest. He continually took us past stinging nettles and mud. We finally thought we knew in which wood he would rest. We hurried ahead to find the perfect high seat. Alas, only a roebuck braved the open ground—no red deer in residence.

Tamás and I were covered in mud, stung by stinging nettles, and laughing about how smart and crafty this old boy really was when we found several sets of large stag tracks leading to and from the corn. Checkmate. We found how the old boy got in and out. Tonight, we would see if lady luck was anywhere around.

Michael took a ten-kilo, fourteen-point stag. Lodovico shot one late that we would definitely have to find in the morning, as there was no light in the forest at 8:30 p.m. We went to the road where we saw the big tracks going back and forth to the corn and set up on a large round hay bale. Two young stags and a roebuck passed at 7:15 p.m.

Surely the old man would soon follow. I could hear at least a dozen stags around me. The real rut was in full swing.

Lodovico told me two more stags appeared in his field about a minute after he took his trophy. Now, Karl had two stags and Michael, Lodovico, and László, my Hungarian friend, each had a stag. I was the last man, not for a lack of trying. Michael would be out again tomorrow, but Lodovico was going to be on his way to Florence.

Ritual

We had a super presentation for Michael's stag that he had taken earlier in the day. Two guides played their hunting antlers to serenade the stag on its final sleep. We celebrated with a bottle of Pol Roger, a little Antinori wine that was crowned with some fine Cuban cigars.

Fallow

On day six at 4:40 a.m., we sat listening to a stag right outside our breakfast window. Michael decided he should now try for a fallow. "OK," Toni and I said.

"But remember, we have only seen a single fallow male with four hunters looking in the woods for days," Toni cautioned.

Michael, who is a determined guy, replied, "All I can do is try."

"Good attitude!" was my immediate, if somewhat skeptical, response.

Tamás and I continued our plan to try and find the guy with the deep voice that kept zigging while we kept zagging.

We now gathered up another guide, Gabor, whom we dropped off in one of the areas where the evasive old brute had been heard constantly roaring. Tamás and I continued to a further spot, where we had also heard his mighty voice. Suddenly, we got a text message on the cell. "Come quickly!"

We moved as fast as we could in the ink black forest and headed back to a path I remembered from one of the other mornings. Instead of getting out of the truck and walking, Tamás did something amazing. He continued to drive into the forest with no lights on. We suddenly came to a full stop in front of a high stand. Gabor motioned that the stag must be in the next field. We could hear him roaring in the open. We quickly, quietly exited the truck and marched across the open field and back into the forest. We were stalking slowly, so as not to alert any watchful female that may be acting as a lookout. I finally peered through an opening just in time to see a big-bodied stag go into another part of the woods. This was the last full day of hunting, and things continued true to form.

Michael took a huge fallow deer whose antlers weighed around five kilos—his second gold medal of the day and third in twenty-four hours. As good as Michael's luck was, mine was exactly as bad. I passed on a big boar, and the only mature stag I saw was a good five hundred fifty yards away at 8:45 p.m.

Before we left, Michael was going out one more time. I had some hunts to go over with Toni, so this stag hunt became just a memory for me. The voice of that elusive stag still roars me to sleep. This was not the first stag hunt I have returned from empty-handed, nor will it be the last, but the allure of the unknown always beckons me back.

Footnote: Lucky Michael took a huge female wild boar the last morning.

A heavy 16-point king of the rut.

Chapter Twenty-Three

A Short Roebuck Hunt

Ruark was the one who famously advised hunters to use enough gun. I would amend that guiding principle by noting that it also helps to use enough jet. Some years ago, during Hungary's opening week for Roebuck, I had a high-quality dilemma. For more than a dozen years, I had always hunted Hungary's opening week for roebuck. One year, though, I had to accompany an important group of premium gun buyers to Italy. They were insistent on visiting Beretta during the opening week of roebuck season.

Tradition speaks for itself.

We flew from the States in a friend's Bombardier Global Express jet that took us directly to Brescia, where the Berettas have worked since the early 1500s. We settled in a beautiful country hotel in Franciacorta, appropriately named L'Albereta Relais & Chateaux. We soon found ourselves in the Beretta factory. The group bought no fewer than seven SO10 shotguns, a pair of Imperial Monte Carlo shotguns, and a Diana side-by-side shotgun. We visited the wood section and carefully chose the best match for each gun. Beretta's head engraver and my good friend, Giulio Timpini, helped me work with each customer. We worked with several other master engravers, who are required to have a minimum of twenty years experience before obtaining the title master. The combination of five hundred years of tradition with the latest technology has no equal in Italy. It was a good day, even if I was missing my roebucks.

Cavaliere Ugo Gussalli Beretta, the fourteenth generation of his family to lead the Beretta company, gave the group a personal tour of his museum. He hosted a lunch where his sons, Pietro and Franco, joined us. It was from this trip that I had the honor to help Tom Siebel, technology entrepreneur, start to build one of the most serious premium Beretta gun collections found anywhere in the world. The rest of the group, which included Duff Baldwin, John Varner, and Michael Groom, all became Beretta collectors and companions on numerous hunts. Our business in Brescia was done sooner than expected and Michael, John, and I decided to head to Hungary for a last-minute roebuck hunt. They certainly had enough gun, and we certainly had enough jet. By early afternoon the next day, Michael, John, and I were in Budapest.

We wasted no time. We drove directly to the Polgar area in the Eastern part of the country. This was not one of my usual hunting spots, but I had hunted a big buck there some years ago and remembered the region quite well. Toni, who seems to know every inch of hunting land in Hungary, told me roebuck antlers were running light this year. Only two outstanding bucks were taken opening week out of thousands recorded. One buck was more than 800 grams. The second was 653 grams. I was pleased that both bucks were taken by a Pannonvad hunter. Several other deer of more than 500 grams were taken. Nothing approached the two top trophies, but we knew from

Author with Tom Siebel, who was building his Beretta collection in Gardone Van Trompia.

our reports that some decent bucks were around. Several of those bucks had outsmarted earlier nimrods thanks to sheer animal spirits or bad aim. It would be a good morning.

I connected on a nice buck, but the others returned to the lodge empty-handed. They saw game but passed on several smaller roebucks. I always feel a bit lachrymose when I am the first to bag a trophy on a trip—but only a bit. I have studied the roebuck in the field over more than seventy-five successful hunts, and I have learned as much from my failures in the field. Sometimes, all that is needed to change the day is a good meal and a serious nap. All the hunters had a different day after that. We saw deer in almost every field we stalked. All three sportsmen had nice bucks before the night engulfed our prey. John took a fine buck at more than two hundred eighty yards in the tall grass.

Michael and Toni saw a super buck the following day, but the goddess Diana was watching. The buck slipped away before he could be properly identified. We all trekked a long way with no solid results to show for the morning hunt. The afternoon proved to be much more productive, as we took two more first-class bucks. Roebucks were moving everywhere.

As the new day quickly turned to night, Michael was to learn why roebuck hunting could be so exciting. After spotting what looked like a good buck from afar, his group located a drainage ditch and made their stalk from within this man-made shelter. Chancing a look at about two hundred yards, before them stood a mag-

A smiling Michael Groom.

nificent buck leisurely eating his dinner. Michael quickly dropped into a sitting position as he held on the shoulder of the deer. A clean shot put him down like a sack of potatoes. As Michael and Pali approached with caution, they both realized the antlers were getting bigger and bigger! But it was the look on Pali's face that said it all—Michael doesn't speak much Hungarian and Pali less English, but they both were able to communicate to each other that this was the holy grail of roebucks. It was a gold medal.

Yo buck, capital buck, grosa buck, and big buck were all descriptions that soon followed by all who studied the trophy. The deer scored an amazing 151 CIC points and weighed 542 grams.

Early the next morning, we drove out to a new area where a nice mature buck was spotted by a guide the week prior. As we marched toward our stand, Imre, my guide, froze. He pointed to a field just past a tree line that must have been a half-mile away. I peered through my binoculars. I could barely make out the head of a shuta, or female, and the rear quarter of a big roebuck. Imre surmised it might be the trophy buck with one of his harem. Easing our way through the first field was no problem, but as we approached the trees, we soon realized the brush was so thick that it would be extremely difficult to reach the pair from this position. We continued a hundred yards or so when we caught sight of a game trail that extended into the next field. We slowly tiptoed through the bush so as not to alarm the deer. At the edge of the field, we noticed a large mound of dirt and proceeded to the top of it to garner a better look. Out in the field was a single doe that kept looking to her left. We could not chance leaving the safety of our cover to figure out if she was watching for her mate, as lookouts can be anywhere. As with almost any species, it is the female who has saved many oblivious males.

Within a matter of minutes, another large deer presented himself out on the other side of the field. While Imre focused on the animal, I happened to glance back in the opposite direction and spotted the first roebuck we had been stalking. He was sneaking off with three females toward the tree line. He was fairly close. I could clearly see his antlers. Imre turned back toward me, catching sight of the buck I was watching, and within a split second the look on his face was telling me to shoot. Now let's see, a moving deer at two-hundred-plus yards from a shooting stick at a bad angle, and I'm to bring him down?! Oh, what the heck! You only live once! I zeroed in on his head through my scope and knew immediately to take the shot before the forest quickly swallowed him up.

Bang!

The old man staggered while running directly away from me. As the shooting sticks fell, I gave him a final round just for good measure. Yes, he was big. I immediately had the same feeling as when I approached my huge stag from Romania many years ago. As we drew closer to the animal, his antlers kept getting longer and thicker. This roebuck was indeed in the same class as my monster stag of Banloc, Romania. Weighing in at 611 grams, this deer was a once-in-a-lifetime buck and one of the largest roebuck taken in Hungary that year.

Our luck continued. John took a medal-class buck. I looked at the deer from every angle. The bucks were supposed to be on the light side this year. I thought John's buck was a 600-gram monster. He proved to be 553 grams. Rounding out the day, Michael showed up with another CIC medal-class buck.

On the morning of the last day, we were out at 4:30 a.m. so we could leave for Budapest early enough to still catch some afternoon sights. Toni left with John in hopes of finding one better buck that was known to frequent an area west of the lodge. I remember John repeating again and again that he couldn't believe the number of deer that were roaming everywhere; that day was no exception, as John added another fine trophy to our bag. He recounted that as his group was walking slowly along a tree line, a doe suddenly appeared before them at about one hundred fifty yards entering the field. A second doe followed, and behind her a huge buck cautiously trailed. John was lucky enough to have found a small branch to rest on just before touching off a shot. There was a quick second shot and a silver medal was added.

In the short time allotted, we had finished our hunt with three gold CIC medals, two silver, a bronze, and a 10 ½-inch killer roebuck during what was a year of light trophies. For whitetail enthusiasts, this is like taking two 180-class, three 170-class, and one 160-class Boone & Crockett class free-range deer in just three days of hunting.

St. Hubertus clearly blessed our little band of hunters, and we honored the animals that had fallen to our rifles in the traditional European ceremony. Hunting guides provided a last meal to the fallen animals. Hunters removed their hats. There was a moment of silence.

We finished our perfect hunt, then headed off for a day of sightseeing in my second city, Budapest.

A 600-gram buck taken by Dr. Marinos Petratos.

Chapter Twenty-Four

The Call of the Carpathians

I was talking to my wife, Debbie, about what it takes to get ready for a Romanian mountain hunt approximately an hour before I was to leave on one. As we checked off the items on the packing list for the last time, it looked as if everything was good to go.

Author with a fine Carpathian chamois.

One really has no way of knowing what goes into the preparation of a trip, never mind the actual packing. Then, there are all the details to work out with the other four hunters in the group. When will each person arrive? Will they need guns? Do they have US Custom Form 4457 to get the rifles they bring back into the States? On each of my hunts, the sportsmen receive a complete packing list. At the bottom of the page, there is information stating if you cannot find something on the list to please call me, and I will tell you where to get it.

The week before my hunt was to begin, plans changed and two guys arrived a day early. Adam Fenton and I arrived on the first day, while Dennis Salerno, the last hunter, came in from Italy late the same night. No problem. Instead of one pick up, I needed three over a couple of days.

Luckily, Adam Fenton and I flew out of Newark, NJ on Friday instead of the day before, when there was a nor'easter, so we reached Bucharest without delay. But even before takeoff, there were issues. While at the Lufthansa station, an agent looked at our gun boxes in a puzzled manner. We quickly answered her gaze. Yes, they are firearms, unloaded, and in locked cases. We also pointed out that we had ammunition locked in metal boxes in the two duffle bags, as well. After calling the TSA, everything seemed okay. Surprisingly, nobody opened the gun cases or asked to see a license. I mentioned to Adam that it was funny nobody had placed gun ID tags on the cases. So Adam inquired whether we needed to open the guns, to which the agent snapped, "If they want to see anything else, they will call you."

"Well, this is Newark," I muttered, "and perhaps they do things differently here than at JFK."

We rolled into Dusseldorf ahead of schedule and were relaxing in the lounge when an announcement came over the PA system asking us to come to the front desk. An airport agent informed us that the police needed to look into the bags. Now I was thinking no stickers, no signed tags inside, and they were probably not checked in on the manifest. We were then escorted in a van to a baggage area where all the suspicious items are stored. After showing the security men our welcoming letter from Romania, we pulled out our 4457s and a couple of New York City and New York State permits. This did not satisfy security. The police were called to look over all of the papers once again. Next, a supervisor was called. He returned a positive answer within five minutes and said we were good to go. Twenty minutes before takeoff, we were ferried to the plane, and a special security van took the guns and ammo to the jet—we hoped. I saw the plane had the front initials of PB, as in Pietro Beretta, so perhaps luck would smile on us a bit more.

We arrived in Bucharest ahead of schedule and had to wait some time before our gate was cleared. As we deplaned and boarded the bus, the baggage handlers began to unload. I commented to Adam that ours were the last on, so hopefully they would be the first off. Sure enough, first the bags with the ammo came out, then the gun cases followed closely behind. We quickly cleared customs and our gun permits were written out with great gusto. My old friend Dani Gligor met us outside.

We loaded up his vehicle and headed out for a two-and-a-half-hour ride to the lodge of Marian Bucur.

As soon as we pulled into the driveway, the guides informed us that Michael and David DeMathews were already out looking for bear. We settled in, enjoyed a nice dinner, and prepared our kit for the morning. Around 11:30 p.m., I was awakened by some low mumbling voices downstairs. It was not the loud noises you come to know when someone returns after a successful hunt. I turned over and went back to sleep. But in the morning, I awoke to some good news. Michael had taken a gold-medal bruin the first night. It is always a good omen to have something in the game bag by the evening of the first day.

The clock read 5 a.m. when Adam and I piled into a truck with three guides for a one-and-a-half-hour drive up into some of Romania's highest mountains. The logging roads were active. Crews were in full swing. We dropped Adam and his guide, Bay-Bay, off first at a location that would give him the best chance for a big chamois. Because Adam had just run a marathon two weeks prior to the trip, we placed him in the toughest spot to climb. George, Florien, and I continued until the road ended by an old logger's cabin. We began to climb on sheep paths that were not hard to navigate. We saw our first animal a thousand feet above us. Now I realized where we had to go to get a chamois. Oh boy!

Adam Fenton and the author with two outstanding chamois.

We watched a small male cross at 467 yards, then several more way up on the top of the mountain directly to the left of us. As we continued our climb, we reached the snow line, where we made out a group of six chamois that were heading into a pine forest at a clip too fast for us to get a good look. Even when we stopped to eat, we scouted the areas with eyes and binoculars hoping to find the group's resting place. Finally, George spotted a male about 800 yards away crossing an open area on the side of the next mountain. We slowly made our way up toward a plateau that would hopefully put us above our quarry. As chamois mostly look down for danger, we would be in a perfect position should they happen to walk out. We continued to climb and climb and climb. While we were having a bit of a rest, a chamois darted out at 267 yards. As he approached 233 yards, I had my rifle at the ready, only to hear George mumble, "Too small, only about 95 points." This would have been a shooter in Slovenia but not here in Romania, the land of the largest European chamois, the Carpathian *Rupicapra rupicapra*. Now the question was if this was the animal we had been stalking just over the hill or if it was it his cousin from down the road. We soon found out the answer, as we finally reached the highest vantage point. Nothing. Nada. Zip. All the climbing for nothing! Oh well, this was part of the game of hunting.

The fog began to set in, and a light rain trickled down. The rocks were steadily becoming slicker. This made for a real challenge for the trip down the mountain. With the help of my BOG walking stick and Gigi—George—we made it down safely. Because of one new knee and a second one a couple years away from the same fate, I needed all the help I could get. Mountain hunting is, for the most part, a young man's game. Yet some of my dedicated friends are still hunting the high peaks well into their seventies. My friend Renato Mirocoli's dad hunted chamois into his eighties.

Mountain hunting takes a special kind of sportsman, one willing to endure any hardship to obtain his trophy. My first European mountain hunt came forty-seven years ago while visiting my sister Greta, who was in Switzerland attending school. During an evening event, I met a doctor who invited me to hunt something called an ibex. I had no idea what that was. I was seventeen and a fairly accomplished long-distance runner. The Swiss Alps proved no match for me. My next mountain hunt came in Ethiopia for mountain nyala almost twenty years later. Then in my early sixties, I hunted chamois in Slovenia and ibex in Spain. For the true sheep and goat hunter, these would be considered warm-ups for Marco Polo, blue sheep, or anything found in the Canadian Rockies.

We headed back down the mountain and picked Adam up on the way. He told me that after a nice little hike in knee-deep snow, they spotted a group of thirty or so chamois. The challenge for him was trying to pick out the right animal with the help of a guide who could not speak English. By the time they figured out which chamois was the best, they found themselves at a distance of six hundred yards. The physical exhaustion of the first day was tempered by our hard-won knowledge that there were plenty of chamois around. We now only needed it to stop raining.

The chamois are all over the next mountain.

Chamois hunters leave anywhere from 5 to 5:30 a.m. and stay out until 5 or 6 p.m. If you are a true masochist like me, you go back out again an hour later and sit in a blind for several more hours hoping a boar or bear will wander by. Bear and boar hunts usually leave around 5 p.m., and stay out until approximately 11 p.m.

Rain was our constant companion. The second day was more of the same, and we headed up the mountain in a constant downpour. We passed at least a half-dozen logging crews. We dodged trucks that happened to be blocking our way. We kept alert for any logs that might come flying down the hill from above. At the end of the road, we first crossed a long bridge consisting of two logs and no railing, which is no small accomplishment when the wood is slick from several days of drenching rain. The first couple of miles hiking up a mountain always gives one a false sense of security. You are walking on a sheep's path set on a slow rising incline. The fun starts when you hit the pines. Then you climb and climb and climb some more. The second day is always easier. The climbing becomes more comfortable as each day passes. We would walk, stop, and glass through our binoculars at chamois higher up the mountains, some right at the tops of the crests. The key is positioning yourself above the animals since they look down for their enemies. We sighted in at least a dozen chamois, none of which we wanted, and slowly descended the mountain.

I hoped some of the guys connected on at least one of their dream animals. Dennis succeeded. He proudly showed his five-hundred-pound wild boar with tusks of twenty-four centimeters. The wild boar of the Carpathians can grow to monster size. The abundant food sources, good cover, and low hunting pressure help big boys grow. Also, Romania has a closed season that aids in bigger game, unlike most of Europe. And if the boar can keep away from the thousands of bear and wolf in the area for five or six years, he will be a trophy to remember.

We all met up for a late supper at 10 p.m. to recount stories of the day's adventures. It was Adam who told us that his only shot on a medal-class chamois was on one lying down in tall grass. Now the question is, do you take the one-hundred-fifty-yard shot at the spot just behind the ear, or do you wait for him to stand up? As Adam had a good rest on the top of his knapsack, he let one fly. The bullet found his mark, and the Carpathian chamois was his. "I am really happy I don't have to go back up again tomorrow," Adam sighed with relief—this coming from a guy who had just run a marathon two weeks prior.

"Tomorrow is my day," I assuredly announced. However, the rain had other ideas.

The rocks on the side of the mountains are like a sheet of ice when wet. You quickly learn to never step on one. The roots in the dirt can be even worse, as the water makes them an even more formidable problem. Despite these hazards, we marched upward past markers that I had come to know over the past few days. The group spotted a nice male at about fifteen hundred yards standing still on the other mountain slope. We quickly planned the best route and headed back down the mountain toward a beautiful waterfall. On the other side of the falls, we climbed back up the slope, stopping every so often to make sure we were on course. Hopefully we would end up within three hundred yards of our quarry. Upon closer inspection, Gigi judged him to be only about ninety-five or ninety-six points. Disappointingly I passed on the old boy, as I wanted a medal-class head with at least a score of 105 CIC.

We continued to travel on the same mountainside until we reached a small picturesque meadow just above the waterfall. What a super vantage point for lunch. The rain even stopped long enough for us to enjoy our much-needed nourishment. I explained to my guides that this view was why we hunt. Nature's masterpiece is here on this plateau above the world. The view has been the same since long before recorded history.

The tops of the highest peaks were already covered with snow. The vivid colors of the grass, stones, and the differing shades of green catch your eye. As you soak this in, sipping mountain water and chomping on an apple from one of the guide's backyard trees, what could be finer than this Romania, which still retains a wildness like it was before World War II?

The sleepy small-town roads are the highways of cows, sheep, and many horse-drawn wagons. However, there are more cars on the road now than during my first foray in the countryside in 1990. When I first hunted in Romania, once you left the main road for the real backcountry, all that could be found were horse-drawn wagons and people walking. Cars were found only on the primary roads, mostly of either Romanian or East German makes. Back then, gas was restricted, but we luckily had a special tourist permit that prevented us from having to wait in long lines at the petrol stations.

The rain was winning once again as we descended from the Carpathians. The one-and-a-half-hour drive back to the lodge always seems longer with no trophy riding along with you. One of the other guides came in a while later and mentioned that a big boar was feeding nearby. Well, who needs rest when you can be out looking for a wild boar? Not me! There I was, walking in the woods, hoping to see that big splash of black in the midst of all the green, brown, and beige of the forest. Suddenly, I froze. Something big and black walked toward me, getting bigger and bigger as it approached. My boar was turning into a bear! As I had my Sako 85 in .300 WSM with 180-grain federal ammo topped by a Nosler partition bullet, I quickly switched off my safety and found a suitable rest beside a tree. "Turn a little more broadside, please!" I begged. After focusing nicely with my Burris 6V scope set at three power, I let my breath out halfway and squeezed one off. The bear jumped a couple of feet off the ground and hunched forward before running off like a scared deer. I knew the shot was a true one. "Now, who wants to go into the thicket with me and find the bear?" I bravely asked, as it was now completely dark.

We looked around for ten minutes or so on the outer edges of the dense forest. Nothing. By now, George had called in two more guides to strengthen our numbers. We counted three flashlights and two rifles in our arsenal. The team ventured deep into the blackness. I found a trace of blood from the bruin's lungs. As I watched the guys move slowly and cautiously through the woods, I realized this had the makings of what we called in the military "a real cluster★★★★."

I motioned to Petre, the head hunter, to back off, as this was a dead bear that we would find in the daylight. When we reached the lodge, I proceeded to tell the boys of my shot and how sure I felt a dog would find him first thing in the morning–that is, if another bear or a pack of wolves didn't make a snack out of the beast first. Up at the crack of dawn, we moved out with six guides, two dogs, and four rifles. After pointing to the thicket where the bear had darted, the dogs were called to search the bush. Within a couple minutes, one of the hounds had him about eighty yards from where the shot was taken. It took the whole gang to drag him out of the thick stuff, so he could be ready for the camera. A nice bear, but not the biggest of the three I had already taken on previous forays to Romania. He was large enough for a stalked bear, by anybody's calculation.

The next evening, David came back from his hunt with much the same story as mine. He had hit a big bear squarely in the shoulder with a .340 Weatherby magnum, producing evidence consisting of good blood and bone mixed together. As no one really wanted to look for a wounded bear late at night, the gang decided to leave him until morning, armed with a crew, dogs, and more artillery. After an early morning search, they found him within one hundred fifty yards or so from the previous night's blast. It was a super gold-medal bear, just what David had counted on.

Now, it was the last official day of the hunt, and I was left with no chamois. Forget sightseeing in Bucharest as planned; I was ready to go back up the mountains again. There was a slight sprinkle as we hit the base of the mountain. By now, the rain didn't faze me, because this was the weather given by Diana the Huntress. So, off we went. Finally, the rain stopped and the sun peeked through the five days of wet clouds. As we were in the middle of a difficult climb, a group of five chamois could be seen making their way down the hill far in the distance. We hoped to position ourselves above them to spot the area where they would eventually reveal themselves. After about twenty minutes, Vasile, a shepherd by trade, scoped a chamois that appeared from a different area than we had been watching. I took my rangefinder out, checking to see what distances would be workable.

With my BOG tripod set in a firm position, I sat comfortably behind it with my elbow resting on a grassy mound. I was ready for business at about five hundred yards. Just about then, the animal changed directions to one that would only bring him in a bit closer. Happily, I had practiced this distance for four straight weekends before the hunt began. There was no rain, no fog, just a crystal clear picture out of my Huskemaw 5-20 power scope. The 140-grain hand-loaded bullet in my Sako A7 was ready for the job. Lance Berman of Utah, who put the package together for me, informed me there would be no trouble hitting a balloon-sized target at six hundred yards—at least that's what he had done two months prior with the rifle. I rested the cross hairs on the front third of the animal, just in the middle of the kill zone. I was amazingly calm after five days of trekking up and down these mountains. I lightly squeezed the trigger and watched him fall back down the mountain into the middle of a rock heap. Vasile and Gigi were yelling. Everyone was hugging, and I think I was in a little state of shock (just a little, mind you).

As I focused my Steiner 10x40 Predator binoculars on him, I thought he looked big enough for me. When Gigi glanced at him the first time, he thought it might qualify as a bronze medal. I didn't care; I just wanted a good male. Even though both male and female horns are scored, I guess I was showing my macho side by wanting a masculine beast. I kept my eyes glued on the chamois. Vasile raced toward the other mountain at a speed only a shepherd born in these Carpathian Mountains could muster. My rifle was reloaded, should the black goat rise again. Vasile soon yelled to Gigi that it was a good one about seven years old. I really didn't care about the size. He was my chamois. We headed down the mountain and met up with everyone, stopping by a stream three quarters of the way down. We took a lot of photos, skinned the chamois for a shoulder mount, and ate lunch in this picturesque setting. It does not get any better than being with fellow hunters in an Eden-esque paradise as the sun starts dissipating clouds. It was as if the Lord was saying, "Well done. I will now let you walk back down the mountain with no rain or fog."

This was the last piece of the puzzle. Everyone got what they had hoped for.

Adam, Gigi, Dani, and the author.

Chapter Twenty-Five

Fallow Deer at the Gates of Mezohegyes

———

When time allows, I like arriving before driven pheasant shoots to hunt big game. I was lucky one year as a bird hunt put us close to the famous Mezohegyes area, which is dotted with grand country houses and stables of famous Hungarian Nonius horses. It is like a page from an old European fairy tale. Brother Alan Romney, who has shared many hunting adventures with me, was along for a chance at a Damhirsch, a German word that expresses the majesty of the animal far more poetically than our fallow deer.

The largest of these beautiful deer, *Dama dama*, resides in Hungary. Hunters come from all over the world in pursuit of *Dama dama*. Several world records have been recorded in Hungary, including the current 6.2-kilo record. Any set of antlers weighing more than 4.5 kilos is a super trophy and more than 5 kilos is a dream. A rack measuring at more than 6 kilos seems almost prehistoric.

We arrived at the lodge early one crisp October morning. Two pairs of perfectly matched Nonius horses stood attached to handcrafted carriages that would be our hunting vehicles of choice for the next several days. After some quick coffee and rolls, we loaded into the carriages to begin our hunt. It was almost 5:30 a.m. when we rolled past ample barns and paddocks, where many of the beautiful horses trotted our way to see who was passing them by. The cold air, combined with

Joe Forestieri with a real monster fallow deer.

the frost and smells of the woods, makes your entire body come alive, even before you see your first fallow or stag. I have always thought this feeling has something to do with our primordial past, before we were the mightiest hunters of all. It is the same feeling one gets around a morning campfire in Africa.

After a short scenic ride, suddenly a few fallow hind appeared approximately seven hundred yards away. We stopped the carriage just inside a tree line to watch the deer move out into the open field. We naturally scoped the tree line in hopes of spotting the big daddy. He came like clockwork, just after his family had given the all clear. The buck was a four-year-old fallow with antlers of more than three kilos. He was shootable for the rest of Europe, but not here where the kings live. I have hunted fallow deer in Spain, Romania, the Czech Republic, and even accompanied other hunters in the United States and South Africa, so I know what is considered to be a trophy in many other areas of the world. In these parts, it's just a fair head. I kept looking at the deer to see if he would get any bigger. We then lowered ourselves down from the carriage for a slow stalk to an old sturdy tree with a solid branch that could be used for a rest. Hopes were high that an even bigger fallow deer would appear to challenge the fearless leader of this little group.

Alas, it was not to be. Only a couple more young deer presented themselves, just far away enough as not to bother the king of the field. My guide, Pali, told the driver to meet us on the other side of the forest, as we were planning to walk through the woods at a snail's pace. As the sound of the mighty hooves was disappearing into the morning, I could smell something in the air that I had become quite familiar with over the past thirty years. It was the unmistakable musk of the red stag. I am always excited by the possibility of seeing other game while on the trail of a particular species.

As we quietly made our way through the dark forest, our guide cupped his hands in front of his mouth and let out a deep, throaty challenge call to any stag within earshot. An old stag immediately answered back. We sharpened our eyes toward the sound and could barely make out the shape of a large red deer with twelve points. He would have been a real shooter if it had not been after October 15, when you no longer are allowed to take stags with crowns. Another fine trophy slipped away into the mist. No matter. Another time, another place.

About a half-hour later, we picked up some fresh fallow tracks after watching roebucks fly past us, one with an antler of just fewer than three hundred fifty grams or so. One set of tracks looked as though they were from a large male, as a fallow can weigh over two hundred and twenty-five pounds. We reached the end of the forest, and out in the field were a dozen fallow deer with a nice buck grazing in the middle of the bunch. He was a fine five-year-old trophy but not our intended target.

In the evening, we walked around the house looking at all of the wonderful trophies of bygone hunts. Even now, I love that memory—strolling the shadowy hallways with Alan, a glass of brandy and our Cubanos for perfect company.

Results of the October rut.

Early the next morning, Pali and I left in the pitch dark to the clicking of the horses' hooves on cobblestone, then to the much softer sound on dirt paths that led toward the home of the monster fallow deer. We reached a small field in the middle of the woods. We left the driver and horses behind and followed a path for the better part of a mile until reaching a larger open field with some nice blinds. We picked one out and were in it before the sun began to break through the moving mist. Alas, a stag and a small boar were our only visitors. Around 8 a.m., I suggested to Pali that we try a stalk in the forest, where the stag seem to be making all the noise. Soon we were in the thick woods, and it was like a Brothers Grimm fairytale with dark shadows, mist, and glimpses every now and then of almost magical animals.

We saw a fallow at three hundred yards with good antlers that appeared to be the correct age. At two hundred yards, he looked like a keeper At one hundred yards, we noticed a deformed antler. We continued toward a stream that flowed down the middle of the large wood,

which seemed like an ideal place for big boys to pass time when not chasing the ladies. They had cover, good food, and water. We traveled onward. I noticed a dark spot further into the woods that slowly turned into a beautiful fallow buck the closer we walked. We

In this illustration, Zoltan Boros captures a beautiful buck.

slid behind a tree. Luckily, the deer was feeding and had no idea of the nearby danger. As we positioned ourselves quickly, I noticed a fine branch just about the right height for a perfect rifle rest. I was on the buck almost upon touching the wood but waited for the final confirmation from my guide. One must make sure of the antlers and the age of the beast. A well-placed shot from my .308 produced a seven-year-old 3.7-kilogram medal class trophy to remember.

Pali walked back to retrieve the wagon so this monarch of the forest could make his final grand exit. We tied him on the back of the carriage, then made our way through the forest that was ablaze with morning sunlight. I spotted a female, then another, then a fallow bigger than mine trotting off into the safety of the darkened woods. Oh well, such is life. I was happy with my effort and already thinking of the next week with all those pheasants and ducks.

As we drove to the lodge, I noticed Alan's carriage had already returned. I figured it was perfect timing—a double on fallow the same morning! Toni walked out of the lodge and congratulated me on my fine trophy. He then informed me that the doctor had just left after treating Alan.

I exclaimed, "Oh no, what will I ever tell Susi, his wife, if he is really hurt?" It seems he had gotten on the wagon in the cool morning

Peter and old boy.

air, so the driver threw a horse blanket across his lap. To make a long story short, Alan was extremely allergic to the dander in the blanket. Luckily, a doctor was lodging nearby and quickly came to his rescue by giving him a shot that put everything back to normal in a short time.

After years of putting hunts together, you learn to become friends with Mr. Murphy of Murphy's Law fame. You never know what unexpected things will happen. Even with the best plans, sickness, lost guns, no game, and missed flights are just a few of the items Murphy can toss your way.

Alan was fine and, after a good rest, came to admire my luck. Several days later, he had his own luck and connected on a wonderful medal-class animal. Now we could put our rifles away, check our shotguns, and meet the rest of the group arriving the next morning in Budapest. But, that's another story . . .

Guides ready to take fallow trophy out the old-fashioned way.

Chapter Twenty-Six

The Land of Capital Stag

I never tire of hearing the roar of a big red deer—the air cracks with the sound of an old stag yelling to others to keep away from his girls. It is always good to be with other hunters who feel the same way. On this hunt, our merry little band consisted of Dennis Salerno, who took a five-hundred-pound boar with us in Romania the year before; Mark Hennessy, who returned to get the red deer that eluded him previously; and David DeMathews, who bagged a huge brown bear in Romania the season before. We moved along the edge of a darkened forest en route to our stands. We spotted a roe doe with a youngster, a good sign that we had not disturbed the tranquility of the vast fields we were slowly approaching. I was armed with a Tikka T-3 with a Burris 3x9 scope equipped with

Bonita Fraim with her gold-medal stag taken with her Sako Deluxe.

a sweet red dot center. The caliber was the deadly .300 WSM. I was using 180-grain federal Nosler Partition bullets—a package that has stopped many boar, stag, and bear on past excursions.

After a bit of a hike, we reached the bottom of the ladder that would carry us up to a vantage point, where we could see and hopefully shoot in every direction. Akos, my guide, spoke excellent English. He said he saw a nice stag roaming this area two nights previously. He had chosen the best stand, which allowed for a southerly wind. As I made myself comfortable, I took out my range finder, pulled out my portable blind seat, and simulated a shooting position from everywhere a stag or super-sized boar may make an appearance. We had already heard about a half-dozen szarvas, or stag, roaring in the woods around us. We were optimistic. During this first night's adventure, we saw a young stag at three hundred or more yards serenading the ladies. I watched him with great interest. A male boar appeared out of nowhere and trotted across the field to our left. He was a two-year-old, which allowed his safe passage until December, when Toni and I planned to return here to hunt driven boar. We heard at least eight stags calling this first evening and intensely discussed which were old men and which were the pretenders to the throne. I was pleased that everyone had heard or seen deer that evening, but the morning is actually the time for red deer, and it has its own tempo.

We were up at 4:15 a.m. We had some coffee and bread. All the hunters were outside by 5 a.m. We were ready to face the day's challenges. I checked to see if it was cold enough for a sweater when I heard the good morning call from three stags roaming around our hunting lodge grounds. It is a sound that will wake you right up every time. We left the lodge on schedule and hit the woods at 5:15 a.m. in the pitch-black morning to listen to a dozen or so stags welcome us to their show.

Deer were sounding off from every direction. We slowly made our way through the forest. We passed miles of open fields and marched to our stands. Before climbing into our forest perches, we made out at least twenty red deer. One was a large-bodied brute, but his antlers were concealed by the lingering night. We quickly climbed up the rungs of the ladder and into the safety of our blinds. As we climbed, more deer were seen in every direction. We could now see seven males and I was thinking one of those babies just had to be a shooter. As the sun illuminated the forest, we noticed one deer had a short antler, two others were too young, and so on. We watched the stags from two stands, and the only shooter never ventured closer than seven hundred yards. We decided to head to another hot spot deep in a forest about five miles away from our first morning's foray.

One never knows what may appear out of the morning mist.

While driving to the new area, two additional mature stags were briefly spotted by the side of the road. As we exited the truck, sounds of roaring stags could be heard from every direction. We stalked to within fifty yards of one singer, but could not see him in the thicket where he had so wisely placed himself. After walking a mile or so, still hearing stags everywhere, we finally made our way to a stand in the middle of the woods, which had fantastic shooting lanes reaching out on all sides. We could hear deer close by—unfortunately all in the deep forest. Then, as if by magic, a mature stag halted at one hundred meters and stood still for a few moments. I saw his right side clearly, which had seven thick points. Now, I just had to see the other side before I could take my safety off. Alas, a broken left side permitted him to pass unharmed.

Some of the roaring stags were now quite close. It was another twenty minutes before the next deer came out, showing his young body. He was about seven years old, if that. We were only hunting for deer ten years or older. The kid was permitted to pass, and it was time to change our approach, as the stags closest to us were changing direction. They were moving off to our left. Our group quickly moved up the hill to the next stand. We only saw two more young stags before deciding to return to the truck. As I turned to watch Akos descend down the ladder, a couple of hinds appeared behind him at about one hundred fifty yards. I motioned for him to stop. We watched at least a dozen more hind and young file by.

I was thinking that in an area full of love-hungry stags, this group had to have a head of the harem not far behind. I aimed my rifle right at the spot where each animal had just passed. Sure enough, a big-bodied stag brought up the rear. He stood in the shadows of a big tree. We could not estimate the size of his antlers. I could already see by the shape of his body and his Roman nose that he was indeed the senior member of the group. As he quietly walked away, I counted fourteen thin points—too small. I was certain this was to be my stag since he came out with a large group of ladies, but I was wrong again. With so many close encounters to relive at the breakfast table, we headed back to the lodge with renewed vigor. Just as I was commenting to Akos that someone had to have shot something this morning, his phone rang. It was Mark's guide, László. It seemed Mr. Hennessy had hit a stag solidly, producing a steady blood trail. They were waiting for a bloodhound to follow its scent. Immediately I questioned whether they were nearby, as I am always game to watch a good tracking dog work. Akos agreed that we could tag along, so we loaded into the vehicle and arrived before the trackers.

The bloodhound started working, and we soon heard the familiar bark that the tracking dogs of Hungary use when they find downed game. The deer was not more than four hundred yards from where Mr. Hennessy took aim.

All's well that ends well when you find your game, but until then, you go through a terrible time of self-doubt. The silver-medal stag was in a deep thicket when the dog found him, so it took us some time to drag him out.

It is funny how you come to learn if a fellow hunter has made a vital hit on game. By reviewing just what he or she remembers at the moment of truth, you figure out what you can expect to find when searching for game that did not fall immediately on impact. I have had to rethink shots I took many times myself, which eventually gives one a sixth sense about the outcome.

I remember smelling the stag long before seeing him down. The smell is unmistakable. It has given me a leg up on many a stag hunt

The last ride.

while stalking this wily beast. We took a ton of pictures of the result of Mark's two-year quest for his hard-earned trophy. Happily, our merry group had something to talk about over breakfast, where we all spoke of the many deer we saw moving in the early morning. We were getting into the routine of stag hunting—up at 4:15 a.m., out by 5 a.m., and breakfast at 9:30 a.m. or so. A nap is taken sometime between 11 a.m. and 3 p.m., then we're out again at 5 p.m. with a return at approximately 9 p.m., and finally in bed by 10 p.m. Your body takes some time to understand what is going on, but the results are hopefully more than worth the effort. A good book, some over-the-counter sleeping pills, and a bunch of magazines help. Writing is one of the other ways I put myself to sleep.

Day Two

It was good to wake and again hear the stags roaring all around the lodge as we left for our next adventure. We sneaked toward our stands as a chorus of stags sang. I love being in the middle of the rut, and few experiences in the hunting world match landing in the center of the full rut in Hungary. Stags are everywhere. On the second morning, we saw twenty-three stags, though here it is important to understand the distinctions. When I say stag, I mean anything with antlers. When Hungarian guides count stags, they only include mature animals, which thus far meant a dozen mature stags spotted over the first few days of the hunt. Of course, hunters are not bird watchers, and coming back to the hunting lodge without game is never pleasant. When it happens, you hope someone else took your luck, as brother Dennis did with a beautiful old deer.

The author and guide Akos with stag taken for Hungarian TV.

We had a camera crew with us filming for a Hungarian television show, and we gave them an opportunity to capture a scene unknown to most. At the lodge, the hunting guides conducted a formal cere-mony for Dennis's stag to pay tribute to the animal and the hunter. The chief hunter played the ancient songs on his hunting horn. The sounds awaken the spirits of all hunters who listen, and we returned to the for-est in the mid-afternoon with renewed vigor and focus.

It was now the middle of the afternoon. We headed toward a prom-ising area. Akos suggested, as it was warm, that we walk deep into the forest and stalk our way to a familiar stand. Within fifteen minutes on the stand, we spotted a hind, then another walking from several hundred yards behind us. There were four or five females with a stag bringing up the rear. I was already in position as the first hind hit the opening. My gun was at the level of where the girls were walking out. I just knew the stag would be mine if I got an OK after the last hind decided to run through the opening. Now would the stag do the same? His majesty walked out, and Akos stopped him with a roar. I smacked him good, and for that I am thankful since my one-hundred-sixty-yard shot was caught on camera and would soon be on Hungarian television.

The stag was strong. He stumbled up a steep hill and disappeared from sight. We waited twenty minutes before we started tracking. I never like to needlessly push game. About a hundred yards up the trail, the super buck was laying by a tree. He was twelve years of age, and his antlers totaled thirteen points. He was a nine-kilo silver-medal buck with black antlers and long ivory white tips—a grand denizen of the forest. It took six of us to pull him off the hill and down to the truck for the stag's final journey.

We had the ceremony for my red deer in the evening so the film crew could have both daylight and nighttime rituals to show the full tradition of the hunt. At night, they light fires all around your animal and surround it with branches. The trophy is given his last supper, which is a small branch. Fresh leaves are placed in the stag's mouth. Everyone stands at attention and the hunting horn sings the deer to his final resting place.

Onward We Go

The quiet benefit of a successful hunt is sleep. Stags are hunted early in the morning. Boar are hunted at night in the moonlight. Of course, getting the body's circadian rhythms to adjust to the tempo of game is more an art than a science. Many hunters plan to sleep late only to rise, as I did the morning after my stag hunt, at 5:30 a.m. This gave me time for a nice chat over breakfast with the film crew, who taught me about the Hungarian outdoor channel. I was more than pleased when Dennis returned to lodge from his morning hunt to report seeing boar with piglets and a couple of nice stags. Mark came back to report that he scored on a fine mouflon ram, and that made my day—and dinner. Our group would now be having mutton quite soon.

Chapter Twenty-Seven

Brown Bear of the Carpathians

There I was, once again, at 4:30 a.m. I had already been wide awake for half an hour listening to several Spanish clients gather their gear and head out for the always-challenging chamois. The largest chamois in the world live in the Carpathian Mountains, which stretch across Central and Eastern Europe. I never

The ever-watchful European brown bear. Illustrated by Zoltan Boros.

really know if it is the time difference or just the pure excitement of knowing that I will be out hunting for European bear later in the day that keeps me restless and alert. I use my sleepless time wisely, setting out my kit and unpacking everything else so all is ready and easily accessible for the rest of the week.

Bear hunting is a later-in-the-day and evening event. You have all day to wait. One really cannot hunt anything else in the morning, as the chamois is an all-day affair that leaves a hunter in no condition to sit in a blind at night. Believe me on this one, as I have been there and done that. The early daylight is a time to read, write, and perhaps stroll into the mountains to get the blood flowing and calibrate the senses. As we were really in the country, there was not much to see in the small—dare I say—towns. However, if time permits, there is always Dracula's Castle and the magnificent Peles Castle, with its unparalleled art collection just outside the hunting area.

Dr. Marinos Petratos was with me again. He suggested that it would be a good idea to go on a long walk into the foothills to warm up for the evening's foray. After a vigorous hike, we happened upon a set of old rundown buildings with broken windows. All the panes had been shattered except one. Dani Gligor suddenly had the brilliant idea—reverting to our misspent youth—to see who could take out that last piece of unbroken glass.

"How childish!" I blurted out as the doctor, Dani, and I all looked for the perfect stone. (If any Romanian police pick up this book, Dani did it!)

We headed back for lunch, a short rest, and a 4 p.m. pickup. After riding for an hour up into the higher mountains, it took another half-hour or so to reach the blind. Now the waiting began. Before it got too dark, we memorized everything in the field that could possibly look like a bear. When the full moon appeared, we had to adjust our eyes to make sure we were in tandem with our guides. First, you must see the bear. If he is a good one, you go to step two and close the bolt on your rifle, which anticipates step three, when the guide confirms the bear's location. Step four is to make sure you have a sturdy rest. Step five, remember to bump nothing with the rifle barrel and turn off the safety. Now that you have a plan, you wait.

Hunting from a blind is not the most exciting form of hunting, but it is the only way to have a decent chance at a bear, wolf, or boar in thick timber. I have taken bear in the open on the side of a mountain and have encountered wolf and boar. Such luck is like winning the lottery. This is something I have discussed with my friend, Petre Gararea, the Head of the Hunting Office of the Forestry Division of Romania, on more than one occasion. He feels as I do—this is the most sporting way to have a chance at a mature trophy.

While sitting in the blind, the wait may be long, so enough layers of clothing are of great importance. I begin with long johns, a wool shirt, a polar fleece, a heavy coat, and long socks, a fur-lined hat, good shooting gloves, and supremely warm boots, ensuring you can comfortably watch, look, and listen.

You never know when a big bruin will appear out of the shadows. The first couple hours, you are feeling pretty proud about how smart you were in your choice of uniform to fight the cold. In the next two hours, the night air sneaks in around you and your lifeless body—yes, you have to practice the art of being very still. By the fifth hour, you are moving your fingers and legs ever so slowly to stay somewhat comfortable. Over the years, I have developed several useful tricks to help in the blind, such as to never look at your watch, as it seems to move backward, especially if you are cold. Try to think of hunting only and the shot you will take. Remember to set your scope at three or four power, and make sure it is focused for what is hopefully going to be a close shot. Your scope must have an illuminated reticule; do not forget to turn it on.

Finally, it was time to head back to the lodge—for tomorrow was another day. It was time to think of a warm truck, a leisurely dinner, and falling into a hunter's sleep.

We returned to the super news that two Spanish clients had taken nice chamois on the first day. I could not help but reflect that I seemed to be the only one who had to spend five days hunting these monarchs of the mountains in the past several years. After admiring the trophies up close and personal, we talked of mutual friends we knew in Spain and shared photos of past hunts into the night. The success with the chamois infused the air at the lodge with excitement and anticipation for the next day's hunt.

Stand hunting is not glamorous. There is no stalking or navigating a trail on the side of a mountain. But stand hunting can have its own reward, such as making your way through a beautiful Romanian forest carefully cultivated and cared for by the hunters and woodsman. Our stand on the second day was like a little house. We settled in and all eyes were glued on the meadow in front of us. Suddenly, to our left something moved out of the woods a couple hundred yards from the stand. Was this to be my bear? It was not. It was a record-class boar standing still—one of those Romanian mountain monsters that weighs a good four hundred or so pounds with big white tusks. Now, if I were to shoot the boar, the bear may hear and head for the hills, but the bear could also be a good kilometer away. I did not like the odds, and since it was not my first big boar, he received safe passage into the night. Passing up a trophy shot is not easy. You may start to second-guess yourself and think of the old homily that a bird in the hand is worth two in the bush.

As you get a little colder sitting in your stand and the night becomes blacker, you will wonder to yourself if your decision was foolish. St. Hubertus almost always favors the patient and the faithful.

Almost two hours passed like this, but suddenly something blacker than the night entered the field and appeared to be coming our way. The guide studied the bruin and quickly whispered, "Bun," or "good." Now, there was one minor problem. I could not see anything through the scope. The crosshairs were lost in the night. The walk back to the truck after you have let the big one go is long, but it is preferable to unleashing a wounded, irate eight-hundred-pound brown bear on the Carpathian Mountains that you must then meet in the thickets for an encounter that will be his last or your own.

The author after a successful stalk.

Even in a distant country where you do not speak the native language, hunters have a common language. Gigi, my guide who helped me take my monster chamois in 2009, told me they knew where to place the blinds because, while hunting chamois with their clients, they watch where bears loiter. Sheepherders, who are not big fans of the mutton-eating bear, also know to tell hunting guides. Loggers and the occasional tourist may also help determine where the best place to erect a stand might be. It is true that you never know what animal you might meet high in the mountains. Dr. Marinos and I saw wolf tracks at about sixty-six hundred feet while looking at peaks that were more than eight thousand feet just across the way. Recently, one hunter spotted a lynx at close range, and I scoped a large mountain stag last year. The biggest-bodied Eastern European stag are those of the Carpathians.

We headed back to the lodge hoping for better news from the good doctor while praying that our chamois hunters did not take all the hunters' luck with them. It was now 12:10 a.m., and Dani and Marinos were not back from their hunt. This is, most of the time, a good thing, as it means they have some game to prepare and haul out. Of course, there are two other possibilities. They have stayed out to get the benefit of a high moon, or a big bear or boar is wounded and hiding deep in the bush. My rule when wounded dangerous game is in the thicket at night is to have a quick look around the outsides of the brush with a couple strong flashlights. If nothing turns up, go home. Bright and early the next day, return with your tracking dogs and three or four experienced guides. I have been charged by leopard and wild boar at night, and let me just say, it is not for the faint of heart. Many people think it is a great—perhaps the ultimate—test of courage and grace under pressure to stand and dispatch a wounded or charging animal. However, these encounters do not always have a cinematic ending. Do not be a hero. Let the professionals take over when a dangerous situation arises.

At 12:40 a.m. I couldn't reach anyone on their cell phones, so my mind began to wander about both good and bad things that go bump in the night. By 1 a.m. I decided to turn in and get the story tomorrow. At breakfast, I heard a no bear story and a lengthy almost story. The doctor explained that after a steep climb to a stand where the guides had seen not one but two males, he and Dani settled in and waited. It was not as cold as the previous night and with no wind it was a bit more pleasant. The moon was full, and the sky was lit by a million stars. Still, at 11 p.m., when another giant of the Carpathians showed up, it was too dark. No matter how the doctor tried, he could not find the mighty beast in his crosshairs. Marinos said he remembered my warning at the start of our hunt to avoid looking for one of those wounded boys at night in a thicket on the side of a mountain. He was fine not taking a low percentage shot. The score was now bears: three and hunters: nothing.

Another day faded as we discussed our latest plan of attack. We take all the guides' information and put it together to decide which blind will have the most light and be the easiest to climb in the dark. In my knapsack was the following: first aid kit, energy bars, water, a space blanket, a camera with extra batteries, matches, extra ammo, toilet paper, and a warm hat. I checked the coat I would be taking, as well. The pockets must have ammunition, warm gloves, a small flashlight, shooting glasses, and some hard candy. Now, all I needed to do was grab everything, along with my rifle and BOG walking stick, and I was good to go.

On your way to your destination, look out for logging trucks blocking your way, crazy drivers that swerve and almost hit you (which happened to us one night), snow, and bad mud after a rainstorm. Beat all that, and you can start your climb toward your blind. If the bear doesn't smell you and you aren't busted by a boar or stag, you can have the privilege of sitting and waiting in a cold stand for five or six hours.

Yet again, I was settled in, rifle at the ready and whispering back and forth with Dani about where a bear might appear. After an hour of watching the hunter's friendly light disappear into the night, we noticed something black moving through the trees and into the field in front of us. It was another monster wild boar, even bigger than the one from the other night. Let me tell you, the Carpathian Mountains of Romania hold some ridiculously large *Sus scrofa*. We saw some long tusks on this denizen of the forest. Big teeth on a large boar make for high gold-medal material. Having judged more than five hundred trophy boar, my call was tusks of at least twenty-two centimeters. Gigi and Dani thought they could be even a little larger. After about a minute of thinking how nice some boar meat would be and what a fine trophy his tusks would make, I let the second wild boar pass and waited for that big bruin we had hunted for five days to zig rather than zag.

The next morning, we took the good doctor up the highest mountain to search for chamois. The only one we saw was at one thousand yards walking the wrong way. Some mornings you see a few dozen males, then there are the other days, such as the one we just experienced, are climbing and climbing with nothing to show for it but an appreciation for a view from the snow-covered mountains across thirty miles of crystal clear sky.

I prepare, once again, in the now all too familiar blind. My rifle was within easy reach, binoculars were crystal clear, and my seat was in the most comfortable position possible. The waiting began yet again. I focused, closed my eyes (forty winks at a time), and played mind games, such as naming all the countries in the world. I can name more than one hundred fifty. I have played this game a lot. Around 9:30 p.m., after watching a total of thirty hours, Catalin spotted a big wild boar parading in the field. These wild boar tend to own any area they desire. A bear will almost never challenge them. An old male boar is a small tank that can keep up with a deer in a short sprint. His tusks can rip anything up with alarming accuracy. I remember in 1991 watching three different bears arrive on bait only after a five-hundred-pound porker decided to move off and let the poor bruins have a go. This is why you only see big male boar lingering around a bear's territory, because they are definitely not afraid of any stinking bear.

Suddenly, a wild boar appeared out of the black forest. It was the large one from the other night. He was a tank. He sported gold-medal tusks and a five-hundred-or-more-pound body. I debated once again. "No, I will not pull my trigger," I told

One never knows what will happen during a bear hunt.

myself. "The bear still might show up." The boar paraded around for an hour or so and slowly marched off for a second time; I had let this prize of a lifetime escape again.

It was now past midnight, and the moon was bright over the middle of the big field. No boar and no bear. We decided to wait another fifteen minutes and call it a night, when suddenly a dark spot started moving from the right of the field. Bear? Boar? Wolf? It was coming our way. It was not the bear. It was not a lone wolf. It was our boy the king of the wild boar, and it was to be his last moonlit walk in the Carpathian Mountains. With a 220-grain Federal chambered into Debbie's Beretta Mato rifle, I set the Burris scope to three power and confirmed that he was indeed the huge boar I had been watching the past few nights. As the old boy walked within eighty yards of our stand, I had him from a dead rest. He turned at a slight angle to me. My memory had seen this shot many times before. I took a deep breath, exhaled halfway, and squeezed off the shot. Smack! We heard the good sound. The boar quickly disappeared to the left into the dark forest.

Dani and Catalin were both sure it was a solid hit. I concurred, but we waited twenty minutes or so to confirm.

I put on my new headlamp and chambered another round. Catalin sported a 12-bore double rifle loaded with slugs. Now the fun really started. We fanned out with the lights glowing and soon arrived at the area in front of a fallen tree where the boar was standing at the moment of truth. No blood, no hair—nothing but the hoofmarks where he peeled out at a scary speed. We all agreed he was hit and that a boar of this magnitude can quickly close a wound. We tracked the wounded boar to the tree line and quickly realized it was the beginning of a steep, seventy-foot drop. After having spent a long time trying to spot our trophy, we proceeded with caution down the slope. This is why I brought the headlamp—one the New York Beretta Gallery had just started carrying. It lights up quite a large area in front of you, while allowing both hands for your rifle.

Suddenly, Dani yelled, "Waidmannsheil!"

I quickly answered back, "Waidmannsdank!"

We had just shared the traditional salute of jagers, or hunters, in Germany.

"Can you see him clearly? Nothing moving?" I asked.

"No. He is quite dead!" Dani shrieked.

It was music to my ears, as the brush was getting quite thick, and it was better to meet this big boy under these more restrained conditions. His tusks and body did not get smaller as we approached—as is often the case, they got larger.

The walk and drive back to the lodge seemed shorter after the night's results. The next morning, we took a number of photographs of this king of beasts to send to Bob Vitro, my taxidermist. I decided that my Carpathian Mountain boar would be a full mount. Of course, I hadn't told Debbie yet, but she found out when she edited this chapter. (I really love you, honey!)

And still there was the bear. After we studied reports on what every guide was seeing, we decided that perhaps the giant bear had moved

Now that's a wild boar!

to the other end of his territory and appeared in yet another field. It was a steep climb to our new digs. It brought to mind vivid memories of last year's chamois quest. We settled in as I memorized everything that could mimic a bear in low light. Around 8 p.m., I began dozing off when Gigi grabbed my arm. It was a slight squeeze that you come to crave on those cold mountain nights, as it meant he saw something moving in the dark.

He pointed to the right, and I could just make out the silhouette of a bear. Alas, upon closer inspection it turned out to be a female, as the bear lacked the big hump along its back—a telltale sign of a male bear. She found something to keep her busy for about a half hour, then began looking noticeably spooked every time she peeked over her shoulder. This is usually a good thing, because it's a sign that something bigger than her wants the field. She looked over her

shoulder and took off as a giant bear was taking over the terra firma.
He looked big in the dark, like a grizzly, but I thought the shadows
of the night were playing tricks. Catalin quickly uttered those magic
words, "OK, shoot!" I was unbelievably calm. I slid off my safety. He
was mine. Just as I was about to pull the trigger, he turned and his
huge head covered the exact spot I was about to unload upon. Without changing my target, I patiently waited for him to lift his head.
He did, and I did, and I heard the magic whack sound and then the
bear fled. We waited the customary half-hour that tends to be long
enough for hunters to avoid any surprises with a bodacious bruin.
I had my gun ready with both my SureFire headlamp and small flashlight shining away. Gigi was beside me with his side-by-side shotgun
loaded with bear-stopping slugs.

There was no need for backup. This almost prehistoric mountain bear
was stone dead at thirty meters from where I shot him. The reality of a
super big bear did not set in immediately. As we approached the old brute, I
could hear by the tone of my two guides' Romanian speech that this was a
special animal. His big head, big bump on his back, big feet, and a big length
all confirmed it. As a matter of fact, everything on this beast was huge, and
his coat was long and shiny after more than a dozen winters. Catalin said

And that's a bear!

it was one of the largest bears either hunter had ever seen. The steep climb down the mountain in the pitch dark was of no concern to me, as my high from the bear would have permitted me to fly down if need be. The next morning, we loaded this nine-hundred-pound plus big boy into the truck and headed down the road where everyone wanted photos of the special bear. Marian, Silviu, Dani, Thea Lemke—whose husband was high in the mountains looking for chamois—and all of the hunting and house crew came to see what all the fuss was about. A million or so photographs were taken using numerous cameras and phones. This was a good thing because in the blackness of the forest, it was hard to get a decent photo. I was lucky that I had the feeling about staying one extra day. The hunter's hunch has served me well endless times.

Those of us lucky enough to hunt again and again learn to trust our instincts. This, coupled with trusting your guide, has been a combination that has brought home many last-minute trophies.

There are so many giant bears around; just ask Michael DeMathews. Gold medal European brown bear, Romania 2010.

Chapter Twenty-Eight

The Great Driven Wild Boar Hunt

While in Hungary filming the *World of Beretta* TV show while hunting roebuck with Chris Dorsey, we began talking about boar hunting. This, of course, led to driven hunting. Chris's eyes lit up on the possibility of participating in a driven boar hunt for the show *Dangerous Game*. As Pannonvad does a number of super wild boar hunts year in and year out, I said, "You're on!"

Dusan Smetana, Chris Dorsey, and John McGillivray after a successful driven boar hunt.

We were talking about two videographers (Thomas Teeter and Jeffrey Scholl), a sky cameraman (John McGillivray), and a still photographer (Dusan Sean Smetana) being able to work in and around a line of ten guns—no easy task. However, as we had more than a year to hash out the details, I knew we would somehow manage.

Toni and I worked closely with Gyula Varga of Sefag. We picked out three super areas and put together a line of real wild boar aficionados. As luck would have it, several months before the trip, Delta Airlines decided not to continue direct flights into Budapest from JFK, so our travel agent, Joyce Striar, proceeded to book us on an American flight that would. Again, our luck was challenged, and American canceled their direct flights to Budapest. Their offer was to fly us through London, which is a place known to be difficult when traveling with firearms. Joyce went to work and found us all a flight on a Lufthansa airline connecting through Munich.

Long story short, our group of five—Chip Brian, Bruce Colley, Alan Romney, Joe Clayton, and me—arrived safe and sound with guns and ammo. We proceeded to pick up our sixth hunter, Ken Noble, in Central Budapest. A few hours later, our seventh gun, Chris Dorsey, arrived, along with his crew of four.

Bill and David Hooks, our eighth and ninth guns, were arriving later, and the tenth gun, Hans Eckl, had already reached the lodge. The first night, we rushed to sight in our rifles before the light was gone. At dinner, I gave my standard safety speech, of course. Safety on a driven boar hunt is paramount, as you have ten people with medium to large caliber rifles on the line. I talked about how to move the gun past the other hunters, where it is safe to shoot, and most importantly, where it is not. Other significant points, such as when to take your safety off and never have your rifle loaded anywhere but in the stand, were ardently stressed. Everyone had a guide to tell them again when it was safe to shoot, as it changes at each stand. He or she would also help with spotting and identifying the animals.

The first day, we could shoot wild boar, hind, fallow deer doe, fox, and jackal. Yes, jackals had in recent years appeared after traveling through Bulgaria and Romania from the Middle Eastern plains. You have to be careful not to shoot a fox or jackal too early, as you could easily turn back a good boar that is not cognizant of the impending drive. The same questions always come up the night before the hunt. Our six guns with driven boar experience helped Toni and me answer many of the redundant questions. We also explained to the group what to carry in your knapsack, such as a knife, flashlight, extra ammo, tissues, water, and chocolate or energy bars. I carry a good first aid kit, as well. The proper clothing starts with long johns, long wool socks, a shirt, sweater or polar fleece, and a warm coat that is water repellent. Besides a rifle and ammunition, one needs good gloves, a scarf, and a hat. Some pieces of clothing should have hunter's orange on it—if not, we provide hat bands. With all of this information in hand, everyone should be good to go!

Even for me, the anticipation started to build as soon as we were on the road. As we arrived at our destination, I saw many familiar faces from the area's head man, Zoltan, to the beaters and dog handlers. Coffee was served while we were being introduced to our guides and going over the safety rules again. Cards were given out that told hunters on what pegs they would be shooting on each drive.

After you are dropped off for the walk to your stand, your heart begins to beat one level up as you realize the hunt is about to become a reality. You look all around your stand to familiarize yourself with where the best shooting lanes are located. Now, a dead silence falls over the forest. Your eyes move slowly through the trees, and you chance an occasional peek back at the cut right behind you. Suddenly, off to your left, you catch a glimpse of a huge boar slipping silently into the forest, then a rifle cracks the air. Now, all your senses go into overdrive.

There, running directly at me, was a mature male with visible tusks. The Beretta 689 in 9.3x74R was up and both triggers were squeezed before I had any time to really think. Down he went within ten feet of impact. No matter what happened in the next several days, I had a successful hunt. As I came back down to earth, I asked Martin, my video man, if he was able to capture the shot.

His answer was, "You could see the impact on the screen." Now the pressure was off. I listened to hear how the others were doing. There was a fair amount of trigger tapping all around my stand. I could actually hear bullets hitting several animals. Another two boar ran to my left. As they were both females, I picked the biggest one, which was perhaps seven or eight years old, and my luck continued.

As the drive was about to end, I caught a flash of a nice boar at about two hundred yards trotting through the woods. By the time

I pointed to Zoltan, the black spot in the sea of brown and green vanished. Soon the beaters came by and pulled my trophies to the side of the road. I look down the line and noticed three other dead boar. We had to stay in our stands until a truck or horse-drawn wagon came by—we do not want a client finding a boar walking down the same path he is on or worse—a wounded big boy finding you!

Ken Noble had been shooting off to my left and it was two of his boar I could just make out once we hit the road. With Ken's first hunt under wraps, the pressure was off of him, as well. Joe Clayton, who had the stand up and to my right, came to tell me he also had a tusker down. The first drive—and the first hunt of the year—turned out to be super! My buddy Bruce Colley from the Mashomack Club had several outstanding boar down on his first time as a member of the line.

Young David Hooks, whom I have known since he was a mere slip of a lad, had the most interesting story of the morning. It seems as he and Toni walked to the stand, a lone boar strolled down the same game trail. Toni told David to wait until he got a bit closer, which he did, but when he threw out a shot, he missed. The angry beast then barreled toward David, who managed by the hair on his chin to clear a fallen tree. The boar smacked that tree hard and sent a major piece of wood flying! Toni yelled out, "Shoot him!" and as the boar turned, a quick shot to the head put an end to the question of any more charges.

It was just that morning that Bill, David's dad, told me two things when I asked him if David was excited about the hunt. His reply was that yes, he was 90 percent excited but 10 percent frightened about being charged. After I made sure David was fine, which he was, I turned to his Dad and exclaimed, "At least the 10 percent is out of the way!"

Everyone had seen boar on that first drive. Just catching a glimpse of your prey and hearing shots can make anyone's day. I talked with Gyula about

The author and head hunter.

where the beaters would be coming from in relation to the next drive. Rumor had it that the local boar liked to hide in a certain big thicket after being driven. To know the movements of game and have stands set up in the correct places—taking into account the direction of the wind—are essential for a successful driven boar hunt.

Chris Dorsey, who was acting as director on this hunt, had also scored a couple of boar that his videographer captured perfectly. This really made me feel good, as all the planning was having a positive effect. The helicam worked overtime trying to capture photos of running boar. This is not an easy task when you are in a forest with narrow clearings that don't allow much of a chance for open footage. For lunch, we quickly ate some sandwiches with hot tea, as we were covering great distances for each drive and the time was passing fast. Why eat when you could be hunting? With rain in the forecast and daylight ending at 4:30 p.m., time's a-wasting!

Most driven boar hunts have two drives before lunch and one or two after. Everyone connected on more than one boar that first day. This was indeed lucky, as even on the best hunts someone can get skunked.

Lord, how the volume goes up at dinner after a successful first day. We now heard the rest of the stories from some of the other hunters who were on the other end of the line. Brother Alan Romney, a veteran of many of my hunts, recounted how one big boy flew by. He put the crosshairs on the beast for the blink of an eye before it disappeared as quickly as it came. Chip Brian, on his second driven boar hunt with us, had several good boar down. The group listened intently as

The morning gathering.

he elaborated on each encounter. Of course, what would you expect, as he was using a Tikka T3 in .300 WSM with a Burris scope? He said the combo really put them down. Hans Eckl from Austria also made a fine shot on a keiler as it was trying to escape across a small cut. Now everyone clearly understood what I said about boar suddenly appearing and at what speed they can disappear, as well.

By now everyone knew the drill on how to be ready for the morning. Everything you wear should be laid out the night before with boots and socks near a chair and guns, bullet belt, and knapsack by the door. As with any kind of hunt, 5:30 a.m. is not a good time to look for anything! Sleep came easy to me after a perfect day but not before I thought back to the beautiful ceremony and well-documented display of our boar and hinds, which were all perfectly laid out by size and sex. The fires shone brightly at all four corners as beaters, guides, and hunters all lined up and listened to the three guides trumpeting the songs of homage to the fallen game. It still resonates in my mind.

The helicam, videographers, and dozen still cameras made memories that few hunters could even imagine.

I would be among the first, as I usually am, to arrive at the breakfast table in the morning. However, it seems that the most committed hunters always show up before the crack of dawn, no matter what kind of hunt. Eating early allows me time to deal with any last minute surprises.

On this second day, we were out at 6:30 a.m. for a drive into the mountains to hunt in the middle of a 9,200-acre forest. As everyone had some success, we randomly placed the guns with Chris and I situated in the more open areas to further the video possibilities. Luck came my way even before the drive started, as a boar wandered past the open lane not eighty yards from our hideout. Once shots attacked the air, I saw red stag, roebuck, and fallow deer sneaking off or running in any number of directions. A big female boar ran past me full out with no chance for a shot. I kept my eyes glued to the opening just in time to catch another good-sized lady boar that tried to escape. This time I was prepared and sent a shot flying. The result was no boar, but a perfect hit on a tree—mind you, that was not the only one hit over the three days. I looked back again to the opening, and sure enough, a smaller male approached. Bang! He was not as lucky as the first two of his sounder, or boar pack. I was indeed in the right place, as I had two boar and a hind down for the morning's effort.

We managed to eat a civilized lunch in a nearby hunting lodge and finished up nicely with some hot coffee and Cuban cigars. I must say, we were lucky with decent weather these first two days. I was never really cold, but I have been on several invigorating hunts when it was snowing with a strong wind at 10 degrees or so. For me, the weather never makes or breaks my hunt. I simply adapt the best I can—I am always good to go! Do not let bad weather ruin your hunt. Make sure to carry in your knapsack a second pair of gloves, a fur hat, rain jacket, and face mask. You must learn to go with what nature hands you.

By now, new friendships formed at the evening's presentation and dinner table. Although we did not take as many boar the second day, the group's spirits stayed high. The last day, we had sun and cool tem-peratures. Everyone had luck, once again, during the first drive of the day. Lord, there were animals of all kinds that tried to make their escape in front of the beaters and their brave little dogs. After three days, the line under-stood this kind of hunt-ing—don't move before

One heck of a day.

you must, pick the best potential shot when more than one animal appears, and spot the game earlier. All these tips help make one a more proficient driven boar hunter.

Ken's wife Masha had been hunting by herself and joined us for a day. Here are her impressions!

Nine Hunters, One Huntress
By Masha Noble

To hunt is a thrill, but to hunt with nine men—well, I guess I went for the kill. Peter, Chip, Bruce, Ken, Bill, David, Joe, Alan, Chris, and crew, I thank you.

Driven boar hunting in Hungary—acres of land, naked trees, all the beaters, the entire boar—they all knew this was to be a winning score. Toni kept us all in check, while Peter made sure his hunters set the American record.

If you are going to do something in life, you'd better do it right, they say. Well, I would say that this is indeed the Peter Horn way. Shoot straight, mind the hare.

We had perfect weather, a perfect line, and a hunt that went right near the top of the list of any I have had the pleasure to attend. Once again, more memories were created and cemented in everyone's stories of the hunt file!

Most of us returned to the Le Meridien Hotel in Budapest for a day or two of shopping and sightseeing. The last night, with cameras still in town, we descended on O'Buda for a farewell dinner to remember. Lord, how the stories got louder and longer as the beer kept coming!

Some big boys.

Chapter Twenty-Nine

The History of the World-Famous Lábod Hunting Area

I have had the honor of hunting the Lábod area of Hungary many times with my partner Toni. My good friend Dr. Varga Gyula has since taken over as hunt manager, and it is time to tell the history of this renowned sporting paradise. It is an important story that shows the impact of stewardship of the land and its denizens.

The red deer has lived in the Lábod region for thousands of years. In 1978, an antler was unearthed from some peat soil that was found to be between 3,500 and 4,000 years old. The crown and general shape of the antlers are similar to the racks found today. The Lábod region was famous for excellent small-game hunting before World War II. At this time, 80 percent of the land parcels were

Alan Romney and the author after another good morning.

owned by big landowners and about twenty-five or so families controlled most of the thirty-mile area. They managed their sporting activities at a high level. Hunting was a major social event. Many of the landowners were aristocrats. Count Széchenyi and Prince Fesztetics had large properties in Iharos, Berzence, and Kaszó on Lábod's southern side. Count Draskovics was famous for managing his Sellye area by constantly improving the hunting and shooting.

The most important early areas managed for hunting belonged to Count Imre Somsich, Count Pál Széchenyi, Count Géza Széchenyi, Count Frigyes Széchenyi, and Count Miksa von Hoyos. Both Counts Hoyos and Somsich had large fenced areas for fallow deer. In the early days, red deer were rarely seen. In the late 1800s, pheasant and duck were bred, while wild duck hunting was excellent on Lake Balaton and other small bodies of water during the right time of year. In 1870, Count Frigyes Nádasy took a gold-medal stag on Imre Somsich's property. It was the fourteenth biggest stag at the Berlin Hunting Exhibit in 1930.

Count Pal Széchenyi's property, located in the middle of Lábod, was famous for small game and roebuck hunts. He liked to conduct circular hunts that used many beaters and twelve to fourteen hunters. In one week, the bag could total 2,000 to 2,500 head, including pheasant, duck, hare, fox, and partridge. The area often produced 5,000 to 6,000 wild hare that they caught with nets. The second most important hunts were roebuck. Count Pál Széchenyi snagged an impressive buck in 1866. The rack was fifteenth on the list at the 1971 World Hunting Exhibition in Budapest. The aristocrats planted special shrub forests, Fácános erdö, to hold game, such as roe and boar. Today you can still find these forests in the Lábod area.

Count Géza Széchenyi owned a magnificent property in Csokonyavisonta, Alexandra Puszta, known for small game and roebuck hunts. He was an internationally celebrated hunter. He traveled many times to Africa, Asia, and America. He also hunted stag in the Szellös forest near Lábod. Zsigmond Széchenyi was also a world-famous African hunter who hunted the above-mentioned areas with his friend Géza. Count Frigyes Széchenyi had properties in Somogytarnóca, Ferenctelep, and Aranyospuszta. He was known for great pheasant hunts and always employed well-qualified professional hunters and foresters.

Count Miksa von Hoyos's properties in Homokszentgyörgy, Lad, and Gyöngyöspuszta had fenced areas for fallow deer. He also raised silver fox. During World War II, the fences were damaged, and the fallow deer and foxes escaped into the wild, which created the basis for the healthy fallow deer population found in the area today. You can still see silver fox mixed with red. They are the offspring of those World War II escapees.

Red deer appeared only in and around the big forests. They took between twenty to twenty-five red deer a year. Then game started to migrate from the neighboring areas of Festetics, Hohenlohe, Zselic, Kaszó, and Sellye. With the growing fallow deer population reaching approximately eight hundred animals, one hundred fifty deer were then taken per year to manage the growing herds.

As the livestock in the region decreased, hunters relocated game animals from other hunting areas. In 1958 and 1959, 80 red deer, 29 fallow, 253 pheasant, and 2,850 hare were transported to the Lábod area to improve the wildlife population. This is known because the Hungarians are expert stewards of the land, and they kept detailed records. Hunting for red deer and fallow were prohibited in the early 1950s, which allowed their numbers to greatly increase. Communism also helped—in the 1950s, many new forests were planted. The socialist style of agriculture developed a perfect habitat and tranquil

Once again, that real wall hanger taken by Harry Hersey.

environment for every animal in the area. In 1955, Gyula Scherfleck took a stag that was number eleven among the Hungarian trophies at the 1956 Budapest Hunting Exhibit. Today big game, especially red deer, is all over the Lábod area. The quality of the new red deer population is now mixed with the famous Western and Southern Hungarian populations. Around 1958, the first wild boar was spotted in Lábod. Fifty years later, as in much of Hungary, the boar population has continued to explode.

Hunting Rights

The Lábod State Company obtained the hunting rights over Lábod from the Hungarian government in November 1957. Dr. László Studinka first managed the area. He oversaw 57,835 hectares, or about 144,000 acres. There were just eight professional hunters during the first year, and by the next year there were thirteen. The red deer population largely increased, as each year more and more medal-class stags were taken between 1950 and 1999. More than 50 percent of the stags harvested were medal-class. The quality of the fallow deer also improved, and strong wild boar can be found in the pine and marshy alder forests all over the region.

The small game population slowly decreased as big game became more important. In the old days, a single outing could produce 250 hare, 210 pheasant, and 65 partridge. In later years, a good day saw 120 to 150 pheasant, 70 to 80 hare, and five to six Hungarian partridge. Partridge hunting ended in 1964 and hare in 1969. In 1970, the company tried to breed pheasant, but the project failed due to an inability to reproduce under natural conditions.

In 1963, thirty fallow deer were introduced from the world famous Gyulaj area, and Lábod began producing some super heads. The newly planted forests became great hideouts for wild boar around the same period. Slowly, Lábod was gaining an international reputation. Thanks to Mr. Studinka's connections, the socialist government gave permission to receive hunters from Western European countries. In 1960, the area built the Petesmalom hunting lodge. Later, a house built by Pál Széchenyi was converted into a hunting lodge with eight rooms. Between 1969 and 1973, several roads were built to open up more hunting areas.

Fifteen fallow deer were brought in each year between 1968 and 1973. In 1975, thirty fallow bucks from Gyulaj were introduced into the east side of Lábod. The strong population became evident in 1983. During the 1980s, a concentrated effort was made to keep improving the fallow. At the same time, the stag kept getting bigger and bigger. In 1967, the famous Auloch stag was taken that became the symbol of the 1971 World Hunting Exhibit in Budapest. In 1975, the average age of the professional hunter was 34. They were all well-educated. This was the third piece of the Lábod success formula, the first being habitat and second genetics. Another piece of the success puzzle was to feed deer during the winter months. With an accessible food source, water, and forests for protection, why would any animal move?

Two keepers displayed in front of the Alexandria lodge.

All the novice professional hunters were first infected with the virus Lábodicus and later became experts in Hungarian game management. This is something I have witnessed as a former professional hunter again and again. Around Lábod, it is most evident that these boys know their stuff.

In 1987, the area tried breeding black grouse. The laying and hatching were successful, but the high predator density ultimately won out.

Foxes, pine marten, and goshawk proved to be the downfall of this noble attempt.

Mouflon was introduced in 1989, and the result is seen today in the numerous medal-class trophies taken each year. The wildcats found today are a result of fourteen animals brought in during 1982. Lábod is also known for the breeding of bloodhounds. Since 1959, the area produced many famous bloodhounds, as well as noted dog handlers. Hunters come from all over the country to learn about these bloodhounds.

In 1986, Lábod organized a competition for professional hunters to show their aptitude as guides. Three-member teams came from everywhere to try their luck. The team from Lábod, of course, walked away with the trophy.

The area constantly strives to improve its hunting quality. It has ongoing relationships with many universities, such as Sopron, Gödöllö, and Keszthely, to update its habitat. In 1994, Lábod won the CIC's highest honor—the Edmond Blanc Award—for the continued efforts to improve hunting and habitat. The hunting rights of Lábod were transferred to the SEFAG company in 2004, making it the largest

The Lábod area has some super driven wild boar.

hunting company in Hungary, with more than 250,000 acres. Today, as in most places in Europe, the area constantly works to stop the damage to agriculture by the ever-increasing number of big game animals. After the fall of socialism, it did not help that much of the land became fragmented. This produced more landowners who were sensitive to this damage. The cost of this can be very high, making it hard for the hunting to be profitable. Lábod always tries to work closely and communicate with the many landowners. With this in mind, in 2010 they signed a ten-year contract for the region's hunting rights.

Trophies

Our clients have taken many outstanding trophies in this hunter's paradise. In 2007, Harry Hersey from Florida took a stag with antlers that weighed 14.38 kilos. In 2009, Michael Groom of California took a fallow in Csöprönd with a head of 5.5 kilos. The list goes on and on, as this is the place of the huge stag and trophy-class fallow, wild boar, and mouflon. Lábod is a name known to every serious hunter of European big game.

There are smoker mouflon around the Lábod area.

Chapter Thirty

Roebuck from Different Angles

When does the thrill of the hunt start? For some, it is with the smell of the morning campfire or pine needles filling the air that signals the chances of a successful day. On this particular adventure, it started with my friend Steven Sears's endless questions about his first roebuck hunt. Bright people tend to ask a continuous flow of questions before, during, and after the hunt.

So, it was with brother Steve, when discussing what rifle, ammo, attire, boots, binoculars, etc. to take to Hungary. This was when this adventure started for me, with the numerous phone calls and emails sent months before the actual opening day of April 15.

There is no time like the first time, to paraphrase Mr. Ernest Hemingway. The excitement I found in every exchange with Steve awakened memories of long ago. Mr. Sears, like myself, is a bit of a historian and is someone who likes to soak up the new surroundings of a country seeped in tradition and history.

I quickly offered to meet him a few days before the other four hunters arrived in Budapest. In this way, we would have time to tour places like St. Andreas and Gödöllö outside of the capital. It has been years since time was allotted for anything but city tours, which I can do by myself by now.

I wrote the beginning of this chapter from my room in the Beretta Hotel in Gardone Val Trompia, Italy, as I had to attend three days of meetings before I could head off to Hungary.

The author with a magnificent roebuck.

Here sparks continued to ignite my excitement, as I had picked up a few Italian hunting magazines that were full of roebuck articles and photos. Not to mention the same about wild boar, which might just spring out of a thicket while you are on a roebuck expedition.

I had just gotten off the phone with my partner, Toni. I had called him to see if the late snow had melted yet, as this was the time that no snow should be on the fields. Well, it seemed the snow had just melted, which caused the roads and fields to be extremely muddy. As some of you know all too well, the mud of the Eastern Hungarian plain, or Puszta, is truly something to behold. The rich earth mixes with the melted snow to make even the best SUV cry for mercy.

As there was still a while before we started, one could only pray it would be a different day one. The only thing we couldn't control was the Almighty's weather.

With the end of winter coming late, the deer were still in herds. This gave the big boys many extra sets of watchful eyes always ready to sound the alarm.

Next, the four other hunters arrived on Air France with all eight bags missing. So instead of driving out to the area for a leisurely lunch and sighting in session, we had to wait until 3 p.m. when the next flight from Paris was due to arrive. A quick change of plans put us at the hunting museum in Budapest and lunch by the lake at Robertson's, then back to the airport where seven out of eight bags showed up. I hate to say that we have had more problems with baggage on Air France than all other airlines put together.

Then we arrived at the hunting lodge in the Guth area. Not only was it famous for roe deer, but also producing several world-record fallow deer.

The wonderful Kisvadászház hunting lodge.

The first morning went to the bucks. The combination of wind, water, and no vegetation put the deer at flight from a half-mile away. At least when spring began earlier, the vegetation started to grow quickly. This gave bucks a false sense of security, as they think they can hide in a foot of cover. Without this cover around, they fled immediately upon seeing a truck or stalking hunter.

I saw about a hundred deer on the first morning but nothing standing still. Floyd and Michael Hatch had the same luck, as well as Tim and Adam Fenton. Steve and I were still in the zero column. We all saw many bucks in each area that might have been fifty miles apart. It is staggering to realize that each field passed has deer in or around it. The first night brought many details of both success and failure. Everyone was excited and full of hunter's hope. The shots were all more than one hundred fifty yards, with some well more than three hundred with range finders to prove it.

A buck weighs forty to fifty pounds and stands a little over two feet at the shoulder. Your target is a small one, to say the least. I also advised my clients to buy some small deer targets to practice and practice some more, both on the range and in the field with a shooting stick, tree, rock, or whatever would steady one's body.

In this way, you are already familiar with most scenarios that may arise.

The next day, nature smiled on us as the wind died down. I started to stalk in forests, as I feel this is when my prey will think he is safest.

The areas we hunt produce many of the top heads taken every year. Heads that may be considered trophies in Germany and Austria are routinely bypassed where we prowl. A good buck's antlers and partial skull start with a weight of 350 grams. A bronze starts at 375 grams, 420 is a silver, and 500 the gold. Each year we take numerous 500- to 600-, and even some 700-gram monsters. If you want to hunt roebuck that are the equivalent to 170- to 220-class wild whitetails, this is the place. I have hunted these little deer in no fewer than seven countries, and nowhere even comes close to the quality and quantity of these trophies of the Hungarian Puszta.

Friends forever, Tim Fenton and Floyd Hatch.

Tim and Floyd are high school buddies with eight children between them, so the stories and jokes are endless. Adam and Michael grew up together, so even more color is added to the conversation, which includes endless stories of past hunts from Kyrgyzstan to Botswana and from Utah to Georgia. It never ceases to amaze me how people can remember exact details of a hunt that happened a dozen years ago. Like Steven said, I guess, it is the quiet time with no other daily distractions when our mind is clear to record everything. This is a fact that almost every new hunter awakens to, especially those with busy schedules. The hunt is your time, which people come back to again and again to relive.

As quickly as the wind died down, our luck changed. I knocked down a gold-medal buck by 6:40 a.m. We went to an area with deep woods and rows of perfectly planted poplar trees. When we drove in, we saw maybe twenty deer, including four bucks before the truck came to a stop. I knew we were in the right place. We had enough light, plenty of tracks, and soft game paths everywhere.

I carried my Sako 85 in 270 with a Steiner 2x10 scope, 10x42 binoculars, and a BOG walking stick. Jozsef, my guide on many a roebuck endeavor, carried a BOG tripod with an extended platform, which I was testing on game for the first time.

We moved slowly through the endless pathways. There were tracks of roe and even some boar everywhere. Suddenly, we saw two females. I stopped and immediately looked for a male counterpart. I quickly spotted short thin antlers through my Steiners. Off to my left, I spied another kichi, or small buck. Our party found the usual suspects: small bucks, females, and a bolkas deer, still in velvet. Now the forest was getting thick as we passed the last high seat. Fresh tracks were abundant, and several belonged to mature bucks.

All of a sudden, as we neared a field, Jozsef spots a Yo buck, or good deer. We froze, but his female saw us and was off to the races. From my the angle, I could see that she stopped just before the woods swallowed her up. I thought that if she stopped, maybe her mate would, as well. He was between two trees just where the field ended and the forest began. I had already seen this shot in my mind, as it was the only place I would have a chance if he did stop.

My rest was a solid branch and both the set trigger and scope were good to go. He was quartering toward me as I ever so lightly squeezed the trigger. It was all over in the blink of an eye. The shot was 161 yards through the trees. As we approached him, his antlers got bigger until he was a gold medal. I hadn't thought that would be in the cards.

This year everyone said the bucks were running light due to the harsh winter and lack of food sources. In a good year, the roe deer antlers would run 10 to 15 percent heavier. Everyone in the group had hunted roebuck or some type of deer on endless occasions, except Steven, who shared his impression of his first big game hunt. Aside from the sheer number of game spotted, the ability to pick a trophy, and the quiet knowledge of the guides, he loved the contrast between the forest, fields, and rustic settings at the lodge with the five-star luxury of the Le Meridien back in Budapest. Of course, making new hunting friends was an added bonus.

The Hatches were back from a successful roebuck hunt with us last year. By now, they were old hands who helped the Fentons understand the game. As the weather changed, their luck did, too, and everyone took a fair number of bucks.

We heard there were boars about in a thick wood. A big boy was seen several times in the past two weeks. Steve won the lottery on who was to try their luck. I volunteered to help with the hunt. The first night, we had an all-too-typical wild boar experience—many long hours in a stand that got colder and colder with each hour. Our only reward was a quick glimpse of a fleeing fox. However, the next day as we roamed the woods, I smelled the telltale musk of boar. We saw fresh tracks of not one but two boar. We tracked them to a river with big mud wallows all around. All of a sudden, black appeared in the sea of greens and browns. It was a large female, but what was behind her? A big boar with white tusks shining away. I froze as Steve and his guide moved up. The last thing I said to Steve was to shoot from a tree if possible.

Well, long story short, he shot from a homemade single shooting stick the guide was sporting. The stick moved just as the boar did. The shot was a bit low. We tracked the boar for a while, followed a good blood trail until the night was out, and saw where he laid down. Now Steve got to spend the night of the hunter—a sleepless one—going over the shot a hundred times or so.

This is all part of hunting.

The next morning, we were out with the first light with two tracking dogs and four guides. After about an hour retracing our tracks from the night before, we found the medal-class boar dead where he had laid down the previous night. Wild boar is something one must have luck to take during early roebuck season. So Steve Sears had the new hunter's luck.

Floyd Hatch, Michael Hatch, Steve Sears, Peter Horn, Adam Fenton, and Tim Fenton with the results of a successful week.

The spirit of this hunt infected everyone in our merry little group. The entire band was in an up mood all the time. People were already thinking of the next hunt. Tim and Adam planned to come back in December for driven wild boar. The Hatches had me put together a family hunt to include hare, pheasant, and duck. And young Steve is ready for the mighty Eastern European red deer. Lord knows I could hunt groups like this full time. As an outfitter, one lives for a week like this. Perfect weather, ample game, and real hunters everywhere you turn.

Chapter Thirty-One

Hunting in Romania with Mr. Lee

This adventure came about quite by accident.

My son Lee called me from Philadelphia (he is at Wharton getting his MBA, thank you very much) to tell me he was going to play for the American team at the World Championship of War Hammer, a board game with a lot of similarities to chess. He said the tournament was held in Novi Sad, Serbia. My hunting wheels started to turn immediately, as not only does Serbia offer good roebuck hunting during the rut, but they also have fantastic wild quail hunts.

A plan quickly hatched that would let Lee off in Novi Sad as I traveled on to the town of Ada in the north. Two roebucks and a lot of quail later, I picked up Lee for our trip to Jambolia, Romania. Here we met up with Toni Török, who had not hunted with Lee since Lee was fifteen and hunting stag and wild boar in Hungary. We next met up with Alexandro Bordea, who found the time to be my guide around running his meat business. Lee's guide was an excellent hunter named Nello, which just so happens to be the same name as my favorite restaurant in New York City to eat anything with truffles. I must say, these guides knew their stuff. Both Lee and I had bucks down the first afternoon. Like in Serbia, we hunted tremendous cornfields with openings neatly spaced between each one. After we drove around these fields for a couple hours, we ended up on a road with a twenty-foot-high open stand at the end.

Like father, like son.

I quickly climbed up in the stand, as I know the drill all too well by now. Toni did the calling, and Alex spotted. As this was the rut, many times you could call bucks in by imitating the sound of a female or a fawn looking for its mother.

After a while, a buck came out of the corn. He was headed away from our stand. Toni called a few times, and this old boy was in love. He came running across the field from seven hundred or more yards away. Now we let him come to fewer than one hundred fifty yards, which should be a chip shot, but he ventured to within one hundred yards. Now we realized he was not stopping. As this was not my first rodeo, I already had my Burris scope set on three power. He went down nicely at about seventy yards. It has been twenty-three years since

Now where did I drop that quail?

my first roebuck hunt in Romania, and let me tell you, the excitement had not dwindled. Lee and I had twenty-two thousand acres to split between us for the hunt, so off we went in different directions—my son with Nello in a Mercedes G-wagon and Toni, Alex, and me in Alexandro's Toyota Land Cruiser. Lee quickly saw bucks, but nothing he wanted. Meanwhile, we called one out of the corn, but he was only three years old, so he was permitted to travel safely on.

We walked to another place where Alex said we should set up our BOG shooting sticks for a try at bucks he knew lived in the area. Alex called, and Toni and I were lookouts. A nice roe came out suddenly at about five hundred yards. Alex called again, the buck came a bit closer, then suddenly changed direction. It was now or never. I squeezed, and he went straight down in the grass—or I hoped so in the half-second my eyes closed. Toni and Alex went into the almost-dark field to find the buck. I heard them talking and still moving about after quite a while. This was not a good sign most of the time. As they were combing the area, I now had time to think of the shot. No, it was good, and he should be in that field. Alex came back for the truck. He said there was nothing around the 250-yard mark. I said to look a hundred yards back, as the buck looked small in the scope. Long story short, 342 yards, confirmed with the range finder, was the spot of the buck's demise.

We had heard a shot about an hour earlier and now turned our hopes to Lee. We ventured a call to Nello to find out that my boy had connected on a very old buck. The story, as my son has told more than once, went something like this: as the heat of the day melted away, roe deer appeared from their afternoon siestas in endless fields of corn. After they called in several different areas that produced only immature heads, they traveled to a stand that Nello knew as one that several good bucks usually hung around. As the sun began to drop, so did the temperature. A welcome breeze came from the west. As they called a buck in from the right, Lee noticed another buck coming in to the sweet sounds of a lady deer. Young Mr. Horn had the gun up on the buck's chest as he saw the big antlers. Nello quickly abandoned the smaller deer and confirmed the other was a shooter.

Lee slowly squeezed the trigger, the buck staggered, Lee shot once again, and the buck fell straight down. My son was taught at a young age that bullets are the cheapest part of the hunt, so if the animal doesn't fall right down, shoot until he does. Now we all met up in the field of Lee's success for photos. I must say I was proudest of Lee's deer and just being able to spend time with my son. It is also a rare occasion to go on hunts with Toni by ourselves. Mind you, we have endless hunts with clients, but it is nice to have no set timetables and only yourself to worry about. After some sightseeing in Timisoara, we headed north for some quail hunting. A two-and-a-half-hour drive later, we arrived at the lodge. The owner of the seventeen thousand acres we were to hunt on said Lee could use his Benelli Legacy. We did not bring shotguns, so this was a pretty big deal because the armory that the guides provided for Toni and me were used to say the least.

Found it!

The next morning, we headed out at about 6:15 to meet up with our three guides and their dogs—one German shorthair and two German wirehair pointers. Although the terrain was exactly like Serbia, the dogs ranged out more like in America. Now I have to tell you two things—these quail fly low and always away from guns. Even Lee, who was a sporting clay champion both in New York state and New England as a sub-junior and junior, had to speed things up to get the hang of this game. We were lucky, as the weather was both dry and cloudy, which was a Godsend compared to the 95-degree sunny days I had just been handed in Serbia.

The first field only produced three quail down. Now I was wondering if the migration was just starting here, but the second field produced more than a dozen good birds. Now we were into it, so Toni, Lee, and I moved slowly through the fields, watching the dogs and only the dogs. With three experienced hunters, the line stays straight, but watching for a fast moving tail or a head going down can give you that millisecond advantage before the bird explodes. As in Serbia, the full migration was not on, and we shot ones, twos, and threes mostly. During the last week of August and the first week of September, the guides say twenty or thirty birds bursting into the air at once is not uncommon.

Lee and Toni shot brilliantly—me not so much—and we had almost three dozen birds in just two hours of actual hunting. Like the guides told me in both Serbia and Romania, please come later if you really want to shoot quail. I am already making plans to take the first Beretta Gallery group into Serbia the last week of August and Romania the following week of next year. By that time, we will have a plethora of birds, and I will have

Another fine day.

the best lodges worked out, as well. Like Romania when I found her in 1990, the lodges of Serbia need some work, but with the help of our excellent agents we should be good to go.

Although we did not get to hunt quail for as long as we wanted in Romania, we were more than able to get the flavor in a short time. We will see about running some quail hunts there the week before the start of stag season, as well. This would make for a unique combination indeed.

Lee, Toni, and I headed back to Hungary for some meetings and sightseeing. Lee and I were more than happy to see the Le Meridien Hotel once again, as we were back in civilization, so to speak. I met with people from our September stag, November driven pheasant, and December driven wild boar areas, as well. I also had time to work with Zoltan Boros, the artist who did the sketches for this book. Lee and I walked the length of Vaci Street, the walking street, saw the museums on Castle Hill, and wandered through a crafts fair that we happened to luck into. Lee spent the next day in the town of St. Andrus, an old settlement with many original shops and artisans in residence. Our guides were Diana and Daniel Török, Toni's kids. We had lunch by a river where they catch the trout fresh everyday. I had my fish with truffles, and Lee had his Transylvanian style. There is no better hunting partner than your own son. He has indeed come a long way since raccoon hunting at five years old!

One of Lee's bucks with last supper.

Chapter Thirty-Two

Firearms

Hunters will always debate what they think is the best caliber rifle and which of the newest ones are preferred on game in Hungary and Romania. Working for a rifle company motivates me to stay au courant on the latest technology—coupled with the hundreds of animals I've taken over the past three decades—so I'd say I have the ammunition to write about the American calibers. Toni has taken well more than fifteen hundred animals during the past forty years, so he is a guru of the European calibers.

Always make sure to use the right gun like this Beretta 455EELL in 470 NE.

I have always sought my information on various calibers, ammunition, and rifles from hands-on people who have been in the field and have trigger time. Professional hunters, game scouts, gunsmiths, and seasoned nimrods are the library of gun knowledge that matters most to me. After twenty-five African safaris, hunts with some of the world's most famous professional hunters, and also some less-celebrated guides, I have learned about the small calibers up to the mighty .500 and .577 Nitro Express giant calibers. The knowledge of professional hunters is important. When I was a professional hunter, I passed my knowledge on to my clients during twenty-five or so safaris. Now, Toni and I share with you our combined sixty-seven years of hunting experiences in two of Eastern Europe's prime sporting countries.

Roebuck

When hunting roebuck, I use rifles chambered in .22-250, .243, .240 Weatherby, or .270 Winchester. If you are hunting wild boar at the same time and only have a single gun in your arsenal, I prefer the .308, .30-06, .270 WSM, 6.5x55 Swedish, or .300 WSM. Simply by changing ammunition, for example, from a 150- to 180-grain bullet, you can hunt any game after checking your gun on the nearest target. The .308 Winchester performs well with 150-, 165-, and 180-grain bullets, while the .30-06 works well with 130- or 150-grain bullets on the little bucks and 180-, 200-, and 220-grain bullets for bigger stuff. For the .270 Winchester, 120-, 130-, 150-, and 180-grain weights work well on everything from roebuck to boar.

As for the actual bullet, there is no end. From Nosler partition and Nosler ballistic tip to the trophy-bonded sledgehammer, the list goes on and on. Each bullet does a specific job.

A Warning

One mistake I see sportsmen make repeatedly is switching ammunition and then hunting, and they wonder how they missed that trophy of a lifetime. It is hard enough to get a chance at a good trophy, so please make sure you know what bullet shoots where. I have taken roebuck with every weight bullet from 55 to 165 grains. The most important factor is shot placement. If you are a poor shot, even the mighty .375 H&H will not help.

Some people prefer lighter calibers, such as the .22-250, because it is a flat-shooting bullet with little recoil. This is a perfect combination for a buck taken far out in a field. When you spot a big boy in the woods or brush, though, it is a different story. The chance of a deflected shot is greatly increased by a lighter bullet. When you go up in bullet weight, the bullet cannot shoot as flat or far, but it will not be as likely to be deflected by a blade of grass or twig.

I once shot a silver-medal roebuck on a walk-up in Scotland with a single slug I had left in my jacket from a previous year's hunt. As we approached a clump of bushes, I thought I saw something large move for a quick second just as the host declared that we could take any legal game we could find. I quickly loaded the one slug I had, so as not to mix it up with the number fives I had been using. Just then, a huge buck bolted from the bushes not thirty yards away. One shot and the old boy was mine, which illustrates my point that any gun might prove to be the right one, and the decision should be completely yours after trial and error.

The new calibers, such as the .25 WSM, .204 Ruger, .233 WSSM, and .243 WSSM, will all take roebuck with no problem. The only negative is if you lose your ammunition, good luck trying to find those calibers in the mountains of Transylvania. It is not going to happen. At forty to sixty pounds, the target area on a roebuck is quite small, so you must know your gun before you go into the field.

The .240 Weatherby Magnum deserves special note, as it is rarely seen in Europe. My good friend Lodovico Antinori is a roebuck fanatic. This is his gun of choice. While shooting with him on his estate in Hungary, I witnessed some incredibly long shots taken with this flat-shooting, hard-hitting caliber.

I used a Tikka T3 in .22-250 for a combination capercaillie and roebuck hunt in Hungary and Romania. I could only take one gun for both trophies, so this caliber was the perfect fit. While a roebuck's distance may reach more than three hundred yards, a capercaillie may surprise you crossing an open meadow at one hundred fifty yards or so. Happily, this decision resulted in eleven roebuck and one capercaillie using twelve shots. Both the gun and Federal ammunition performed exactly as expected. The only shortcoming I found with this caliber, as I mentioned before, was shooting into the thick stuff.

On one disappointing occasion, I stalked a huge gold-medal roebuck at one hundred or more yards walking in some thick brush heading toward the forest. As I thought of the 55-grain bullet and the 50 percent trophy fee for wounded game, I decided to pass on the shot. This buck was taken three days later by one of our German clients. His antlers weighed 657 grams, one of the largest taken in the world that year. Sometimes you win; sometimes you lose. I still stand by my decision, and by the way, I took my own gold-medal buck four days later.

In the early years of hunting in Hungary and Romania, I used only a .270 Winchester for every kind of game. I really knew that gun, and with a 130-grain Federal bullet, I managed a good number of roebucks. After practicing constantly at one hundred, two hundred, and three hundred yards, I knew just where to place the crosshairs on those little bucks of the Hungarian Puszta. In more recent years, I have used the .308 and .30-06 for roebuck on several hunts that included stag, wild boar, and fallow deer.

Stag, Fallow Deer, Mouflon, and Wolf

For medium-sized animals, there are a plethora of calibers, old and new, that are adequate to use on the above game. The .270 Winchester, .30-06 Springfield, .308, and 7 mm Remington are just a few of the old faithful.

As I previously mentioned, I began hunting Eastern Europe with a .270 Winchester, and I took everything from roebuck to big stag with the same gun. With the proper bullet weight, I also managed several large wild boar. The .30 calibers are always a fine choice, and ammunition is readily available throughout Europe. If you bring some new gun that takes a cartridge unknown in Europe, you will not be shooting your gun if the airline sends your ammunition to Omaha and your rifle to Bucharest.

The .30-06 is always a good choice because so many bullet weights are available. On one spring trip to Romania and Hungary, I took roebuck, wild boar, and brown bear all using my .30-06 and three different bullet weights.

I am fond of an old family pre-'64 Winchester lightweight in .308 that I own. This gun has performed flawlessly on numerous expeditions. There are many 7 mm calibers, such as the 7mm-08, 7mm Remington Magnum, 7mm Weatherby Magnum, 7mm STW, and 7mm Remington Ultra Magnum that work well on almost all the game in Europe. The reputation these bullets maintain, especially for mountain hunting, is well deserved.

Wild Boar and Brown Bear

The fact that a great number of wild boar and brown bear have been taken with smaller calibers is something you do not want to attempt to prove if you can help it. For wild boar, a .30-06, 7mm, .338, .300 WSM, 9.3x74R, and .375 H&H are the way to go. If you are only hunting boar, heavier calibers with bullets of 200 grains and higher are what I like in the chamber because they break bone and stop animals in their tracks.

When pursuing the brown bear, a .300 WSM, 9.3x74R, .338, and .375 H&H will stop a mad bruin. This is a good thing when you realize that the Romanian bear of the Carpathian Mountains can be one of the most aggressive brutes of his species.

Chamois

When mountain hunting, make sure you really know your gun and what it is capable of doing. Because a flat-shooting, hard-hitting caliber is required, hunters tend to shoot a .25-06, .270 WSM, .280, 7mm Remington Magnum, right up to the .30-378 Weatherby Magnum, which is excellent for long-range shots that hit with the force of a sledgehammer. One thing you must remember about the big Weatherby is that the recoil is not for the faint of heart.

Speaking from experience, I can't stress enough that you must familiarize yourself with your gun and scope before you begin a hunt. On one trip to Slovenia, I borrowed a rifle and missed two chamois before I learned how to shoot it. The gun had a short length of pull, hard trigger, and an old scope. This was definitely not the trifecta for successful chamois hunting. It took me five more days to find my chamois.

The gun I now use is a .270 WSM Tikka T-3 Synthetic with a serious Steiner scope that is tricked out just for chamois. I practice target shooting at distances from one hundred to five hundred yards at least two to three months before any mountain hunt. You will want a light rifle with a comfortable sling for maneuvering around the mountains.

Once again, I cannot emphasize how important it is to know your weapon and to practice, practice, and practice some more.

Shotguns

Shotgunning tends to be a rather personal choice. As I have sold thousands of shotguns here is what I say works: A 12 gauge for all around shooting in Eastern Europe. Perfect for pheasant, duck and hare. For driven pheasant, a pair of 20 bore will work quite well. I like an autoloader like our Beretta 391 and A400 on flighted ducks as they can be high volume at times. For dove and quail both the 20 and 28 gauges are perfect.

Our favorite rifle for driven wild boar, the Beretta 689 in 9.3x74R.

Chapter Thirty-Three

Tourism in Romania

A poet once observed that it is good to collect things, but it is better to go on walks. I think this is particularly true for hunters. It is important to make time before or after a hunt to see the extraordinary sights available in the beautiful countries we visit for sport and to understand the culture and history of places that call to us as surely and strongly as the sounds of game.

The always-present Carpathian Mountains.

Romania's modern history is filled with turmoil. Over the centuries, it has been invaded. Transylvania was under Habsburg, Ottoman, and Walachia rule, though they remained autonomous. The many different invaders all left their marks on Romanian culture.

Romania is a year-round tourist destination. The best time to visit is mid-April to the end of October. Summer can be hot in the southern part of the country, but the mountain resorts and towns in the higher elevations are pleasant during these months. Winter can be cold, and snow is common in the mountains from December to mid-February. This, of course, is the perfect combination for the country's many famous ski resorts.

The people of Romania have a well-deserved reputation for being both exceptionally friendly and hospitable. I have found them to have a great sense of humor, as well.

Bucharest, the country's capital, is known for wide tree-lined boulevards and superb Belle Époque buildings. The city has a reputation for the high life. I especially enjoy walking along Calea Victoriei, Bucharest's oldest and most charming street. You can see the Cantacuzino Palace, the museum of Romanian music, the military club, and the national history museum, which are just some of the delights one finds on Calea Victoriei.

The Royal Palace Square and the National Art Museum are must-see sights. You feel the city's wonderful charm as you enter the old city center, around the area known as Lipscani. In the 1400s, merchants and craftsmen—Romanian, Austrian, Greek, Serbian, Armenian, and Jewish—established shops in this section of the city. This great mix of cultures can be seen in the architectural styles from baroque to neoclassical and art nouveau. The area has been revamped with art galleries, antique shops, and coffee houses. At the center of this section are the ruins of the old princely court, built by none other than Vlad Tepes, or as he's better known, Vlad the Impaler, who inspired Bram Stoker's *Dracula*. Bucharest has thirty-seven museums, twenty-two theaters, two opera houses, and three concert halls. Many are architectural attractions by themselves.

The shops in Bucharest afford everything from antiques to handcrafts. There are many truly original crafts, such as embroidered clothing, painted eggs, pottery, icons, and rugs. The artizanat, or handcraft stores, are found throughout the city. The nightlife in Bucharest is diversified. Eighteenth and nineteenth century palaces house elegant casinos where guests can play many games of chance, dance all night, and dine at sumptuous buffets.

Peles Castle.

If you have extra time, make the seventy-five-mile trip north of Bucharest to Peles Castle, which is nestled at the foot of the Bucegi Mountains. Peles is a true masterpiece of German new-renaissance architecture commissioned by King Carol I in 1873. The castle has one hundred sixty rooms filled with historical artifacts. It is worth the trip to see the crystal chandeliers and German stained glass windows, not to mention the fine porcelain, ebony, and ivory sculptures.

Transylvania: The Legendary Land Beyond the Forest

Transylvania has numerous medieval towns, spas, quaint villages, and a wealth of historic attractions. Some of the best-preserved medieval towns—most notably Sighisoara, Brasov, Sinaia, and Biertan—are located in Transylvania. Tourists marvel at unique architectural treasures while strolling down the narrow cobblestone streets. The region is home to almost two hundred villages, churches, and fortifications founded by the Saxons between

Vlad Tepes, Prince of Wallachia.

the thirteenth and fifteenth centuries. Transylvania is best-known to westerners as home of the central figure in Bram Stoker's *Dracula*. Romanians have quite a different view of this legendary nobleman. Vlad Tepes is considered to be a great hero by his fellow countrymen. He defended the country against the invading Turks in the mid-fifteenth century. You can visit Dracula's castle—Bran Castle—or see Poienari fortress in the village of Arefu, where many of the legends, including Vlad the Impaler, are still told.

Bucovina's Painted Monasteries

One of Romania's painted churches.

Among the most picturesque treasures found in Romania are the painted monasteries in Bucovina. You are instantly transported back in time by the brilliant blue of the frescoes, the beauty of the countryside, and the friendliness of the chanting monks. The illustrated biblical scenes, prayers, and historical themes displayed on the outsides of the buildings served as visual Bible lessons for the masses that could not read or had to remain outdoors during crowded services. Perhaps the place I remember best from this storybook area is Voronet Monastery. The quality of the frescoes and vivid blues, known as voronet blue, are truly something to behold.

The monastery is located near the town of Gura Humorului in Southern Bucovina. Stephen the Great, the ruling Prince of Moldova, founded the town in 1488 to fulfill a pledge to Daniil, a hermit who had encouraged him to chase the Turks out of Walachia Moldova. Voronet's exterior paintings were created in 1547. It was a working monastery until the beginning of the Habsburg rule in 1785. It became a religious retreat once again after the fall of communism in 1991.

There are many sights to visit throughout Bucovina that are too numerous to mention. Again, if time permits, this region is another must-see.

Maramures

This region in Northwest Romania is home to many villages where century-old traditions are still part of everyday life. As it has for hundreds of years, the social life in Maramures revolves around the village church. UNESCO has recognized the wooden churches in Surdesti, Plopis, Rogoz, Barsana, Budesti, and Desesti as important world heritage sites that are unique in shape and ornamentation. The high roofs and table-narrow pointed steeples are often described as the gothic-styled Maramures.

The region is also known for numerous carved wooden gates. I have often shared a dream with Debbie about my idea to have one of these beauties installed in front of our lodge, as they seem to continuously haunt me. These calling cards of the local woodcarvers are supported by four columns, which are profusely carved with traditional motifs, such as the sun and twisted ropes. Both symbols signify life and continuity. You must also stop at the cemetery for a look at the colorful grave markers. Each color has a different meaning, and the inscriptions tend to tell not only the good things, but a person's imperfections, as well.

If you want to see Romania as it was more than a hundred years ago, this would be the place.

Crisana and Banat, the Historic Gateway to Europe

The first region I ever entered was Western Romania. It was the spring of 1990, and in twenty-four years, I was the first American allowed to hunt near Timisoara. We entered through Arad and hunted

Pischia, Sarlota, Banloc, and Cheveres. Toni seemed to know everyone in the game department, as he had gone to school or worked with everyone we met.

I was checking out the area for future hunting possibilities with Toni and our newly formed hunting venture, Pannonvad. We participated in many television, radio, and newspaper interviews expressing what we thought of this region and Romania in general. I remembered saying that I had found not only a hunting paradise, but also a tourist destination filled with smiling faces. This region may not be as well-known as Transylvania or Bucharest, but it is worth a closer look for the serious traveler. The history-rich Crisana and Banat are steeped in old cultural traditions and a diverse architectural heritage.

Timisoara was the first city I ever visited in Romania. The abundance of Secessionist architecture has given the city the nickname of Little Vienna. When I first saw Timisoara in 1990, it was emerging from twenty-four years under Nicolae Ceaușescu. It was quiet and tired. Today it has a cosmopolitan beat all on its own. There are year-round musical and theatrical performances, art galleries, museums, and a buzzing nightlife.

You should see the ruins of the Timisoara fortress, Dicasterial Palace, Banat Museum, and of course, the Museum of Fine Arts. Western Romania is a great place for active travelers and adventure seekers. There are abundant opportunities for trekking, mountain climbing, hunting, fishing, horseback riding, and more. Crisana and Banat's natural scenery and good climate hold some of the best-hidden treasures in all of Romania, such as the Bihor Mountains, where you can explore caves, underground waterfalls, and hidden lakes.

One place of special note is Chiscani, also known as the Bear's Cave, named after fossil traces of cave bears that went extinct fifteen thousand years ago. I might mention here that their relatives are still around the mountains of Romania and are quite large, to say the least. Other towns in the region I have visited are Arad and Oradea, which I pass through quite often coming and going to Hungary. Oradea has more than one thousand religious sites of different denominations. Arad can trace her roots back to the twelfth century. You can see both the influences of the Austro-Hungarian empire blending with the traditions of old Romania.

The Blue Danube: The Green Delta and Black Sea

Six hundred seventy miles of the Danube River run through Romania before pouring into the Black Sea. The Danube forms one of the most spectacular wetlands in the world. The Danube Delta is considered the world's third most biologically diverse area, after Australia's Great Barrier Reef and Exundas Galapagos Archipelago. The area is filled with tree-fringed lakes, many islands, marshes, and oak forests. There are more than 5,400 animal and plant species found in the Delta.

The mysterious Danube Delta.

This remote roadless wilderness makes you feel like you have reached the end of the world. Boasting a size of 1.68 million acres, this wonderland has endless possibilities. The duck and geese hunting are stupendous during the migration. Monster wild boar inhabit the islands and grow really large, as the bear and the wolf are not invited.

One of the best ways to see this part of Romania is to take a cruise. The Iron Gates, Constanta, Tulcea, and Giurgiu are just some of the sights you can see on your way to the Black Sea Resorts. If you have time, spend a few days at the Mamaia-Rex Hotel on the Black Sea. From here, you can take a cruise to view the other sights along the sea.

Not having traveled everywhere there is to go in Romania, I have probably left out some super destinations, but if you are an adventurer at heart, as all true hunters are, the places I mentioned should keep your eyes open and camera clicking.

Chapter Thirty-Four

Tourism in Hungary

On my first trip into Hungary in the mid–1980s, I drove from Florence through Italy, Austria, and on to Budapest. The name of this city brought magical thoughts to my excited mind. As a history major, the cities of Buda and Pest were names I knew well, but to actually be there was a different story. The history of this area goes back more than two thousand years ago in Óbuda in the Northern part of the city. A number of Roman ruins are to be found in the town once named Aquincum.

Looking at the Castle Hill district of Buda from the Pest side.

This was both a civil and military area, which includes two amphitheaters, villas with superb mosaic works, a bathhouse, and an aqueduct.

The castle district of Buda was erected in the sixteenth century and rebuilt in the Baroque style four hundred years later. The palace at Szent Gyorgy was the royal residence of the Hungarian monarchs for seven hundred years. Today, it is the home of Budapest's most frequented museums and art galleries. I especially love the Hungarian National Museum, which houses a spectacular history of art in Hungary from the tenth century to the present. You can see collections of early medieval and renaissance stone works, gothic wood carvings, renaissance and baroque art, and nineteenth and twentieth century paintings. Here, one may inhale the full flavor of Óbuda. Sections of the medieval royal palace in Buda, the chapel, and gothic sculpture have all been restored.

The Fishermen's Bastion, a neo-Romanesque bulwark with seven towers built on a medieval foundation, will offer an excellent view of the city. I always try to bring my groups to the area for not only the sights, but the shopping and restaurants, as well.

You must travel down Andrassy Street, as it runs into the Hero's Square. I especially love the group of Magyar Chieftains and the statues of the kings, generals, and politicians that run along the pillars. On either side of the square, one finds two world-class museums. The Museum of Fine Arts, which houses the largest collection of Spanish masters found outside of Spain, and the Palace of Arts, located across the way, always holds interesting exhibitions, as it has the longest exhibit hall in all of Hungary.

One of my favorite stops is Vajdahunyad Castle, which is right off the Square just past the ice-skating rink. This imitative anthology includes some of the old Hungary's famous building and architectural styles. Of all the buildings in this area, the most important to me is the replica of the Castle in Vejdahunyed in Transylvania, which is today part of Romania. It houses the agricultural museum, the first of its kind, which was established in 1896. In this museum, you will be amazed at the fine collection of hunting trophies and weapons dating back a thousand years. There are panoramas of all the game of Hungary, and several world-record heads always seem to get a long look from my groups.

Pest also has many historic districts and famous sights. The state opera house is a must-see, and the performances are world-class. Several architectural styles from Romanesque to Classical can be seen throughout Pest. The Hungarian National Museum and the Jewish Museum with Europe's largest synagogue both show the diversity of Hungary's one-thousand-year history.

Margaret Island is an interesting stop in the Danube River. It is a scenic island of peace and quiet. No cars are allowed. Outside of Budapest, you will come to the Danube Bend area. With towns like Szentendre, here you will find old Hungary and super shops, folk arts, and handmade items from throughout the country.

Visegrad is a town known for the breathtaking palace of King Matthias (1458-1490). With three hundred fifty rooms and two-tier fountains of red marble, the palace will leave you breathless. Don't miss the ruins of the Roman military camp from 330 AD or some of the forest restaurants near the game preserve.

Other cities to see include Esztergom, Vac, Rackeve, and Gödöllö, where the Baroque Royal Palace of Franz Joseph and Queen Elizabeth stand.

Eger

The Eger wine region is located in the Bükk Mountains that stretch across the northern part of the country from the Danube to the Tisza. The village of Hollókö is secluded among the ridge of the Cserhát hills. This medieval town was the first village ever declared a world heritage site by UNESCO. There are fifty-eight buildings in the center with a whitewashed storybook church in the middle. Please do yourself a favor and visit the thirteenth century castle on top of the hill, which offers a super view of the old village and her surrounding landscape.

Eger is a thousand-year-old Episcopal and archiepiscopal seat that is one of the most beautiful baroque cities in Hungary. Here in 1552, a handful of Hungarians fought against an extremely large Turkish force. The town has a proud heritage that can be seen in her numerous museums. You can sample and buy some excellent wine, as well. Try the famous Bull's Blood Vino, then take a dip in the natural hot springs on the outskirts of nearby Egerszalók. In the Aggtelek National Park is one of the world's great geographical phenomena, the Baradla stalactite. The cave runs for almost twelve miles, and tours are given according to one's physical abilities. The park has many rare species of both flora and fauna that, along with the caves, make for a worthwhile excursion.

Tokaj

The Tokaj wine region has been producing the king of wines and the wine of kings for more than four hundred fifty years. The old wine cellars are something to behold. The Rákóczi alley has twenty-four tunnels and can store huge quantities of wine. The famous wine of Tokaj got its start as a medicine in the middle ages.

Additional areas to see include the towns of Sárospatak (with many remnants of the Rákóczi dynasty), Sátoraljaújhely (the country's northernmost town), and the Zemplen Hills (where you can see golden eagles, wolves, and lynxes).

The Puszta

The famous Hungarian grey cattle on the great plain (Puszta) in Hortobágy.

Hortobágy is home to Europe's largest expanse of grassland prairies, the Puszta. Here you can find Hungarian grey cattle, stud horses, racka sheep with spiral-shaped horns, and buffalo roaming all over. The famous Nonius horse has been bred here for more than three hundred years.

Lake Tisza

You will love the smooth water, huge bays, and islands rich in fish and game. There are beaches and resort towns found all along this

127 kilometer body of water, which is second only to Lake Balaton. The thermal waters at Tiszacsege are always a perfect 81 degrees centigrade. With various protected areas, there is a great diversity of fauna and flora. The old inn at the Meggyes Csárda Museum is one of my favorite stops, as it takes you right back into a history long gone. Karcag is a typical market town where you can find pottery makers working alongside quick-fingered lace experts. Near here, you can also see the only windmill left from sixty that were in service in the nineteenth century.

Debrecen

This quaint town was known as Calvinist Rome in the sixteenth century. The main church seats three thousand people, and the denomination's influence can be seen all through the city. The oldest hotel in the country, the Aranybika, or Golden Bull, is still open to guests. The great wood, or the city park, is wonderful—complete with a zoo, amusement park, and botanical garden. The thermal waters in Nagyerdo are famous for helping with arthritis and sufferers of worn joints.

Szarvas, or Red Deer

As you drive into this town along the Koros River, you are greeted with the Arboretum, or Pepi Gardens. There are more than sixteen hundred kinds of trees and bushes, including many rare species. I also enjoy the working gristmill and the old Slovak house. The river offers many species of fish that should not be missed in the local restaurants. We often stay in this town during some of our driven shoots.

Szeged

With many hours of sunlight, the city is aptly named The City of Sunshine. There is no shortage of churches in this town. I love the Reok Palace and the synagogue with an art nouveau-moorish style. This city is home to the famous pick salami and Szeged paprika brands. So remember to stock up on these goodies before you leave.

A Hungarian shepherd with his Bunda (sheepskin coat), used as his house and bed.

Gyula

With flowers, rose gardens, parks, and romantic promenades everywhere, this is the place to relax. The town's symbol is a fifteenth century brick fortress that is the only lowland fortress still standing in central Europe. The castle baths are some of the finest found in a country that is well-known for its baths. A great final visit would be to the farm museum a short ride away to see nineteenth- and twentieth-century peasant life. Just close your eyes and slip back into a simpler time.

Chapter Thirty-Five

Gear and Equipment

Exactly what to take on a hunting or shooting trip is an oft-debated subject. After doing the same type of shoots and hunts in Eastern Europe for more than twenty-eight years, I think my packing lists are pretty complete. However, each year I ask my clients if I have left anything off, and even now, new items are added each and every hunt.

Besides obvious items such as guns, ammunition, and clothing, we include what papers one must have and what extra cash to bring for tips and so forth. Something as simple as a copy of the front page

A well-dressed line.

of a passport has saved more than one hunter from spending extra days in Bucharest or Budapest waiting for the US Embassy to provide new credentials. I always have an extra copy of everyone's passport information, along with gun facts, hunting licenses, and flight details. Things such as cell phone numbers that work in Europe and US contact details are all kept with me on hunts, with copies in New York City and the Budapest office.

Once again, you have to be on the constant lookout for Mr. Murphy of Murphy's Law fame—anything that can go wrong, can and will go wrong. To ward off some potential disasters, I will name a few things we do to keep everything running smoothly. Because we provide the ammunition for each hunter on bird shoots in Hungary, we watch for those who show up last minute with anything other than a standard 12-gauge and take care of the situation immediately. We bring along extra over-and-unders to the areas for pheasants, and an extra auto or two for the duck fields. Several rifles are always taken along with the proper ammunition on big game hunts, as this is a must. Guns can break or may not make it off the plane on time, so we try to cover every scenario.

If a gun breaks or does not arrive with the rest of your luggage, your hunt still goes on. I leave extra clothing and boots, along with anything else we manage to accumulate from trip to trip. You will notice we have included several packing lists that we use for specific trips. There are many basics, such as eye and ear protection, metal gun cases, and a separate ammunition carrying case to satisfy the airlines. Things such as a small flashlight are a must for walking into a blind at 5 a.m. or down a mountain as the sun quickly disap-

pears. An alarm clock would be useful for those who don't respond well to a heavy hand knocking on your door at 4 in the morning! A good knapsack to carry everything you need for a day— and hopefully not for a night in the field—is a definite necessity. On some lists, I try to add a touch of humor to see if people are paying attention, such as packing a mallet and six sharp stakes for your hunt in Transylvania.

Layering is most important on hunts. You can always take a jacket, polar fleece, hat, or gloves off as the weather dictates. The proper foot-wear is something that can make or break your trip. Be sure your boots are

My partner, Toni, always looks the part.

well-worn before you arrive. The weight, height, and fabric of the boot are all to be considered with great care. Things like a good hat or cap are important—make sure it's one that will not fall off every time it hits a branch or when you pull the trigger! The hat should also be warm for the winter and air-conditioned for the summer.

On big game hunts, quiet fabric is a must. Since long underwear is a personal matter, find what will work best for you. I used to swear by silk, but now there are numerous synthetics that work just as well, if not better. The right socks are important too, as you must know which thickness works best for the type of footwear you will be using. Le Chameau boots have always been a favorite of mine on driven shoots, and the proper sock for these are either a long cotton sock for spring or a long heavy wool for fall with a silk undersock for January. It is a good idea to bring along a pair of loafers for after the shoot, as the boots usually come off as soon as you hit the front door of the lodge.

I like to shoot in a vest whenever I can. In colder weather, I start with thermals, a heavy shirt, light sweater, and if need be a polar fleece, all topped with the vest. I love the freedom the vest gives me over a bulky coat. In warmer weather, I just wear a lightweight shirt and the vest.

For clothing, you need the right fabric with the right weight. I have certain shirts for different times of the year and different kinds of jackets and sweaters that seem to do the best job from season to season. In Europe, one does not wear camo. Greens, beiges, and dark plaids for more formal shoots are the accepted colors. Breeks are standard for driven pheasants, but you can switch to long pants for the duck days. Some Americans have something against wearing breeks; however, they are comfortable and easy to walk in. They make getting your rubber boots on and off much easier, as well. Whether you are on a chamois hunt or a on a walk-up for pheasant, you can move and climb

Joe Clayton is always dressed to kill.

much easier in these babies. I have breeks in lightweight cotton for the start of the hunting season (roebuck in April), and in September I change to moleskin, light wool, or heavy cotton. For the mountains from November to December, I switch to wool and loden.

Once you get into driven boar or late-season pheasant, wear whatever keeps you warm. Here is where good gloves come into play. The warmer, the better. I like to wear a scarf or face mask as a shield against the bitter cold, two pairs of socks, and the warmest boots possible. The worst thing that can happen while on a hunt or shoot is to have cold feet. Hand and feet warmers are a must.

Your knapsack or carryall should have—besides plenty of hand warmers—an extra pair of gloves, a thermos with a hot drink, water, a power bar or two, a flashlight, and a small first-aid kit.

I like a good shooting stick, such as BOG, that can double as a walking stick. If you do not have a stick, look for a rest, rock, tree, bale of hay, or fence—all will do quite nicely. However, as you may come on the chance-of-a-lifetime trophy in the middle of an open field where there's no place to rest your gun, a good shooting stick will always save the day. Make sure your guide knows how to put the stick in place quickly and securely. Practice setting up with him or her a couple of times before you go out that first day.

A good shell bag that holds a lot of ammunition is a must. Nothing is worse than running out of ammunition halfway through the best drive of the week.

On a true double gun driven shoot, you need a matched pair of guns. A true pair is two guns made exactly the same weight, length, trigger pull, and so forth. These guns are expensive and are for true aficionados. I have sold pairs from 422,000 dollars down to 10,000 dollars and everywhere in between. Like anything else, it is what you are comfortable paying. Another option is to buy a pair of production guns that will do the job. You do not want a pair composed of an over-and-under and a side-by-side or two guns with different safeties and weights. Shotguns are not like rifles. Most experienced shots can pick up any decent bolt-action rifle with a good scope and produce suitable groups on a target with a bit of practice.

I like to bring my own rifle with a scope and trigger pull that I know gives me confidence. I have rifles that function as a part of me, which would be hard to find in a rented gun. Get to know your gun. With each new rifle I buy, it goes to the range with me at least three or four times before a hunt. I usually have my buddy Charlie Conger, Manager of the Mashomack Preserve Club, sight my guns straight out of the box. Charlie is one of the finest rifle and shotgun shooters in the country. Recently, he had to call and rave about a Sako 85 Bavarian in 6.5x55 Swede. I gave him this beauty to try with Federal 140-grain ammo. This tack driver produced half-inch groups at two hundred fifty yards. After Charlie does all the work, I take the rifle and adjust it for my eyes. I then test drive it from shooting sticks, tree branches, small hills, and anything that qualifies to help for the most important part of the hunt. Once again, I test the gun upon arrival at the hunting area.

At a young age, a relative told me that all you need to hunt is a gun and bullets, which is true, but the other stuff makes things easier. I wonder what my old uncle would say about a range finder or today's shooting tripods. If anyone can think of something we have left out, please send me a note.

Hungary—Roebuck Packing List

1. Rifle
2. Ammo (in a separate metal case)
3. Metal rifle case
4. Binoculars
5. Seat (soft)
6. Shooting stick (I have used BOG brand tripods with much success)
7. Knapsack
8. Eye and ear protection
9. Boots (good for walking)
10. Socks
11. Underwear
12. Hunting pants or breeks
13. Hunting shirts
14. Hat
15. Jacket (preferably good for rain)
16. Shooting vest and sweaters
17. Ammo holder for belt
18. Belt
19. Pants, etc. for town
20. Nice shirts
21. Camera and accessories (charger, extra cards, etc.)
22. Invitation letter (from Peter)
23. Small gifts for guide (hats, shirts, knives, flashlights, etc.)
24. US Customs Form 4457 for guns (for those bringing guns)
25. Medicine
26. Sunglasses
27. Small flashlight
28. Reading material
29. Passport, airline tickets, cash, traveler's checks, etc. (any overages must be settled before leaving Hungary)
30. Alarm clock
31. Toiletry kit
32. Phone with European charger
33. Photocopy of front page of passport (keep separate)
34. Sighting-in targets

35. Converter
36. Range finder
37. Small first aid kit
38. Tissues
39. Knife

Romania—Chamois and Bear Packing List

1. Rifle with sling (ammunition in separate metal box)
2. Metal gun case
3. Cleaning kit
4. Eye and ear protection
5. Warm shooting gloves
6. Warm shooting cap or hat
7. Rain jacket (for knapsack)
8. Warm jacket
9. Shooting sweater
10. Hunting shirts (7 or 8)
11. Hunting pants (3 or 4 pairs)
12. Long socks (6 or 7 pairs)
13. Good mountain boots
14. After shooting loafers
15. Knapsack
16. Medicine and toiletry kit
17. Sunglasses
18. Small flashlight
19. Warm vest
20. Small knife
21. Sports jacket
22. Regular shirts (3 or 4)
23. Underwear
24. Regular socks
25. Regular pants (2)
26. Reading material
27. Passport, airline tickets, cash, traveler's checks, etc. (all bills must be settled before leaving Romania)
28. Small first aid kit

29. Alarm clock
30. Shooting stick (good for hiking in mountains)
31. Camera, charger, and extra cards
32. Inviting letter (those bringing firearms)
33. Customs registration for firearms or receipt for gun showing ownership
34. Scarf
35. Mallet and six sharp wooden stakes
36. Range finder
37. Binoculars
38. Long johns
39. Energy snack bar and water bottles
40. Converter
41. Polar fleece
42. Hand warmers
43. Knife

Hungary—Stag Packing List (September)

1. Rifle (ammunition in separate metal box)
2. Metal gun case
3. Cleaning kit
4. Eye and ear protection
5. Shooting gloves
6. Shooting cap or hat
7. Rain and warm jacket
8. Shooting vest
9. Shooting sweater
10. Hunting shirts (5 or 6)
11. Breeks (2 or 3 pairs)
12. Long socks (3 or 4 pairs)
13. Rubber boots and good walking boots
14. After shooting loafers
15. Knapsack
16. Medicine
17. Sunglasses
18. Small flashlight

19. Hard candy
20. Small knife
21. Sport jacket
22. Regular shirts (3 or 4)
23. Underwear
24. Regular socks
25. Regular pants (2)
26. Soft rifle case (if room)
27. Reading material
28. Passport, airline tickets, cash, traveler's checks, etc. (trophy fees must be settled before leaving Hungary)
29. Copy of inviting letter (we will provide)
30. Alarm clock
31. Shooting stick (I love BOG Products)
32. Camera, charger, and extra cards
33. Cell phone and charger
34. Hunting pants (2)
35. Range finder
36. Binoculars
37. US Customs Form 4457 (to bring rifle home)
38. Sighting in targets (stick on)
39. Converters
40. Ammo holder for belt
41. Toiletry kit
42. Knife

Hungary—Driven Pheasant Packing List

1. Pair of shotguns
2. Rifle (ammunition in separate metal box for big-game hunters)
3. Metal gun case
4. Cleaning kit
5. Eye and ear protection
6. Shooting gloves
7. Shooting cap or hat
8. Rain and warm jacket

9. Shooting vest
10. Shooting sweater
11. Hunting shirts (5)
12. Breeks (2 or 3 pairs)
13. Long socks (3 or 4 pairs)
14. Rubber boots
15. After shooting loafers
16. Knapsack
17. Medicine
18. Sunglasses
19. Extra chokes and choke wrench
20. Small flashlight
21. Hard candy
22. Small knife
23. Sport jacket
24. Regular shirts (3 or 4)
25. Underwear
26. Regular socks
27. Regular pants (2)
28. Scarf
29. Long johns
30. Slacks (2)
31. Shell bag (100-150 size)
32. Soft gun case
33. Reading material
34. Passport, airline tickets, cash, traveler's checks, etc. (any overages must be settled before leaving Hungary)
35. Copy of inviting letter (we will provide), local hunting license or gun permit if available
36. Alarm clock
37. Shooting stick
38. Camera, charger, and extra cards
39. Phone charger
40. Hunting pants (2)
41. Pocket Knife

Romania—Big Game Packing List

1. Rifle with sling (ammunition in separate metal box)
2. Metal gun case
3. Cleaning kit
4. Eye and ear protection
5. Shooting gloves
6. Shooting cap or hat
7. Rain jacket
8. Shooting vest or warm jacket
9. Shooting sweater
10. Hunting shirts (6)
11. Breeks or hunting pants (3)
12. Long socks (4)
13. Rubber boots and good mountain boots
14. After shooting loafers
15. Knapsack
16. Medicine and toiletry kit
17. Sunglasses
18. Small flashlight
19. Hard candy
20. Small knife
21. Sport jacket
22. Regular shirts (3 or 4)
23. Underwear
24. Regular socks
25. Regular pants (2)
26. Reading material
27. Passport, airline tickets, cash, traveler's checks, etc. (all bills must be settled before leaving Romania)
28. Old hunting license or gun permit if available
29. Alarm clock
30. Shooting stick (good for hiking in mountains), such as BOG
31. Camera, charger, and extra cards
32. Inviting letter (for those bringing firearms)

33. US Customs Form 4457, registration for firearms or receipt for gun showing ownership
34. Scarf
35. Mallet and six sharp wooden stakes
36. Range finder
37. Binoculars
38. Phone and charger
39. Knife

Conclusion

By now you should have a world of knowledge on hunting in Hungary and Romania. The actual chapters about different hunts I have gone on in the past twenty-eight years or so should have given you a good look into the unique hunting paradise I found there.

After years of African Safaris and shoots in the British Isles, my youth was awakened again here in Eastern Europe. On each new hunt, I found a rekindled sense of adventure. The plethora of famous hunters, game departments, people, and politicians I met along the way helped me with the two years I devoted to this work.

With the chapters about gear, guns, history, and tourism under your belt, you should now be as excited as I am each time I step off the plane in Bucharest or Budapest. This part of Eastern Europe truly has its own flavor. The game management is top notch, ensuring you have a chance at a spectacular trophy. Everyone involved on your hunt are hunters who are happy to have you as their guests. Although the accommodations can range from castles to small lodges, the people of the countryside will do their best each and every time, wherever you rest your weary bones. Once you get out of the big cities, life becomes much simpler, whether it is the flat plains, hills, forests, or mountains, and you will feel the magic in the air.

You should plan the time of your hunt to coincide with the best time to encounter each animal. The middle of April for roebuck in Hungary because hunting in Romania starts in May, so you can combine both countries on a single hunt. September is the time for the stag rut, which moves east as the month progresses. October brings the rut out of the fallow deer and is also the time of the mouflon. Bear hunting is good in April through May and in October, as well. Chamois is best in October and November if the snow does not come too early. Wolves can be found during bear and chamois hunts or may be encountered unexpectedly during any big game hunt. Wild boar can be hunted anytime in Hungary, but the fall and winter produces the best skins.

Although Romania has a season for wild boar hunting, fall and winter are the best! Driven boar in both countries is tops in December and January. Driven birds in Hungary are good in November and December, with January providing the most challenging birds. Flighted ducks also provide great sport in October into November, but you have to watch for the lakes freezing over. The year 2011 was the last year you could hunt capercaillie in Romania due to logging and other invasions into their territory. Make sure you plan your hunt with a company that is present in these areas all the time, as some areas are far better than others. Only by being constantly on top of the best possibilities can outfitters provide you with outstanding hunts. This is why I primarily stick to a couple of countries where I have people constantly in the field.

If I go to other countries, such as Argentina or Spain, I use the same tried and true people again and again. As an outfitter, you must be important to the area, and they will always make sure both you and your clients are kept happy.

Plane fares are very different if you do not have an agent who is constantly booking all classes of tickets into Eastern Europe. For hotels, I keep sending my people back to the ones that have taken excellent care of my group for decades, such as Le Meridien in Budapest and the Capsa in Bucharest. They welcome hunters and are used to arranging tours of hunting museums and the best sporting stores.

If you have any questions about these countries and the sporting treasures they hold, please do not hesitate to contact us:

Peter L. Horn II
c/o Beretta Gallery
718 Madison Avenue
New York, NY 10065

Direct: 212-583-1864

Email: phorn@berettausa.com

Or in Europe:

Toni Török

Pannonvad Kft

2083 Solymár

Erdö u.24

Hungary

Cell: 011 36 209 435 654

Email: pannonvad&@pannonvad.hu

Website: www.pannonvad.hu

Hunting has changed in much of Europe during the past fifteen years, and it is changing even now as the European Union exerts its authority over rules, hunting seasons, and even the species that can be hunted on the continent. A hunter's paradise still exists in Romania and Hungary. Those ancient nations are among the last frontiers of an oasis that will not last forever. I would plan a hunt to one of the last frontiers as soon as you can. As the countries have joined the EU, changes might blow into the east from far-away Brussels.

Remember, it is never too early to start hunting.

My Guilty Pleasure

I love this earth,
It's just like candy...
And Hungary is my guilty pleasure.

Walking, stalking,
Sitting, climbing,
All for a glimpse of that hidden treasure.

Fields of sunflowers,
Forests thick with brush
Mountains so high and mighty,
All a space of wonder.

Peaceful silence,
Roaring darkness,
Crackling leaves,
And herds of glorious thunder.

Smells of the fresh morning air,
Sounds of music playing everywhere.
Tastes of special royal meats,
Touching tributes to honored treats.

This is nature's game;
The measure
Of your pleasure
In it's treasure,
Hungary is the name..

Deborah Langley Horn

Index